Poisoned pens

Annie McDowall

First published May 2012

ISBN 978-1-4717-0888-6

*What could possibly go wrong on a residential creative
writing course on the lovely Isle of Skye?*

With grateful thanks to Chris Bolton, Tamara Essex,
Lennart Pesonen, and most especially, Lorna Smith.

This story is a work of fiction. It is the absolute
antithesis of every inspiring writing course or event that
I've ever experienced, and is dedicated to those
wonderful writers who so generously share their time,
their talent, and their passion with those of us at the
beginning of our journeys.

Chapter 1

Welcome to the Skye Creative Hub read the sign at the bottom of the drive. Tessa Birnie swatted a midge from her neck and continued the short, steep climb to the house, dragging a small case on wheels behind her. She had packed sparingly: four changes of top, a thong for each of the days she'd be teaching here. Tessa's slim Apple i-book fit snugly in the case, along with a phial of Jo Malone body lotion and a spiral-bound notebook in which she'd planned her tutorials for this five-day retreat. She would be teaching with Sean Delancey, and he'd be relieved that she'd done all the planning. Sean was one of the more amenable writers, and although he had as big an ego as any male writer in his early thirties, Tessa had found that he was happy to let his co-tutor plan the structure and content of the course. She had brought no novel for bedtime reading: she was wholly focused on her own work in progress. Even though her second and third books had not caused the sensation of her first, she burned with confidence that this book, a futuristic satire on the dog-eat-bitch aspects of the publishing industry, would rocket her once again to the bestseller list. There'd be little handwritten cards beneath shelves in Waterstones across the country, exhorting readers to buy *her* book, even if they bought no other all year. Amazon would recommend it to millions. Tessa's bank would stop sending her computer-generated warnings about unauthorised overdrafts. Her life coach, Zak, had helped her to envision this glorious future (*if you think it, Tessa, it'll happen*), and Tessa felt a slight upwards pull at her mouth whenever she visualised herself autographing a mountain of shiny new hardbacks, surrounded by fawning fans.

Max Logan was the last person Tessa expected, or wanted to see as she stepped into the house; but to her dismay, there he was, lounging over the front desk, hair flopping in front of his eyes while he conversed with the mousy looking girl sat behind the desk. Max had a talent for making conversations look conspiratorial.

"So I'd make it worth your while if you'd give me the double room overlooking the garden," he was saying to the girl.

"I'm really sorry, sir," she replied, "but that room's been reserved for Ms Birnie."

"Ah, but I got here first, and my need for the king sized bed is greater than Tessa Birnie's, know what I mean?" parried Max, leaning even closer towards the girl, who had started to gnaw at a fingernail.

"I'm sorry, sir…"

"Well, look who it is. Max Logan," said Tessa, as she approached the desk. "Up to your old tricks of intimidating the staff? Take no notice, Megan." She aimed this last comment at the girl. "I always have the garden room when I teach here, so Mr Logan will have to make do with somewhere else. Sorry if it cramps your style, Max."

Max drew himself up and frowned at Tessa. "You don't mellow with age, do you Tessa?" he said, with an almost imperceptible emphasis on the word *age*.

"Here's your room key, Mr Logan," said the girl, seizing her chance. Max snatched it from her and strode towards the east wing, favouring Tessa with one long glare.

"I thought I was teaching with Sean Delancey," Tessa said to Megan. "What's Max Logan doing here?"

"When Mr Delancey found he'd been short listed for the Man Booker, he cancelled his teaching engagements," replied Megan. "It's caused us no end of trouble. We were lucky that Mr Logan was available. Didn't you get Marcus's e-mail?"

"No," said Tessa, "And I'm not happy. Max Logan's work hardly qualifies as literature, does it?"

"I couldn't comment, Ms Birnie," said Megan, who rather enjoyed the author's mystery series set in Watford. Although she would never say as much to Tessa, she'd not managed to read past the first three pages of Tessa's last novel, and the first, which had earned positive reviews in *The Observer* and won a minor award, had left her, and in fact her entire book group, cold.

Tessa climbed the stairs to her bedroom. She knew the way well, having taught fiction courses at the Skye Creative Centre for the past four years. No more teaching tedious summer schools at run-down inner London colleges to supplement her work as an editor at the small, struggling press that was still awaiting the manuscript that would make its fortune. As Zak had told her, she deserved better. She deserved to be *here*, on this lovely (if midge-ridden) Scottish island, heading for the best room in the house. She parked her little case by the huge bed and walked over to the bay window, smirking with satisfaction as she gazed over the lush gardens and down towards the ornamental loch. *I'm worth it,* she whispered to herself. And she determined not to allow the unforeseen presence of her ex-husband to take her focus away from teaching an excellent course and resolving some of the trickier passages of her new novel.

Max carried his holdall up the stairs to the second best room. How on earth would he survive a whole week with Tessa? Their marriage had been short and brutal. Max had celebrated each of the six anniversaries of their divorce with a hearty steak dinner washed down by the best St Emilion that he could afford. Tessa had believed that meat was murder, and she had frowned upon his liking for good wine. He dumped the bag on the single bed and noted the dull view over the gravel drive from his window. For a number of years, his regular summer job had been at Vibrant Waters, a Buddhist centre in Somerset; but the management had changed, and Max didn't like the new constraints. No smoking anywhere in the grounds. No alcohol on the premises. A strict demarcation between men's and women's quarters. It was worse than any youth hostel he'd known, and the food was relentlessly vegan. So here he was, his second visit to the Skye Creative Hub, only to find himself co-tutoring with an ex-wife he loathed, and accommodated in quarters reminiscent of college halls. Still, as he watched the students arrive from his window, he was pleased to notice more than one girl he wouldn't mind squeezing into his Spartan bed. Maybe the week would be bearable after all, so long as Tessa didn't spoil it all.

Chapter 2

The eight students made an oddly mismatched group as they arranged themselves around the vast refectory table for supper. Two appeared to be in their seventies, three were women of a certain age, and there was a little cluster of young hopefuls. The septuagenarians, one a woman with roughly sheared grey hair and a tartan skirt, the other a reedy man with a hooked nose and a hearing aid, pulled out chairs and sat at one end of the table. A slender young woman swung a leg over the bench on the opposite side, and the other young hopefuls, a pale young man with a haunted look and a gangly woman in her early twenties with protruding teeth took their places either side of her.

"Mr Logan!" cried a red-haired woman, swinging a chubby leg over the long bench. "How wonderful to meet you in the flesh!"

Max shrank from the mass of warm, ample hips, lime green viscose, and enormous plastic jewellery that had plonked down beside him. She was wearing an overly sweet perfume that caught at his throat. There was compensation, however, in the fact that he was opposite the young hopefuls, and would have an uninterrupted view of a luscious looking girl's cleavage throughout the meal as long as nobody blocked it with the water jug. She was delicious, he thought, admiring the tumble of ebony curls, the generous lips. There was something vaguely familiar about the bucktoothed girl to her right, and he tried, to no avail, to remember where he'd seen her before. She seemed to know him. She'd greeted him by name as they'd filed into the dining room, and now she threw furtive little glances his way; but Max couldn't think where they'd met, and he didn't remember her name. He went back to studying the girl with the dark hair and soulful eyes.

Tessa glanced across the table and followed Max's gaze. She reached across the table for the jug of water, which was a particularly large pottery vessel, lifted it, and then, with scientific accuracy, placed it carefully back down, a few inches away from where it had been.

Bugger, thought Max.

"*Blood in the Mall* was the book that got me thinking I could write," Max's broad-beamed neighbour continued. "I mean, if *you* can find success writing about Watford, then surely there's hope for *me* writing about Croydon!"

"Mm," said Max, wondering whether the girl was a 34D or DD. He tuned out his neighbour's chatter about suburban murders and strained to listen into the conversation taking place between Tessa and her neighbour, a smart woman in a tailored silk blouse.

"May I ask what you're working on?" Tessa's neighbour was asking. "I'm Ros, by the way."

"My current novel is set in a publishing house some time in the future," said Tessa. "The protagonist is a writer battling to get her book published in an era when the Islamification of the UK has taken hold and women are imprisoned for writing. All women have to wear veils, and they are totally subservient to men. Women have a habit of disappearing without trace."

Typical feminist rant, thought Max. Some women just couldn't accept that they might not be God's gift to literature.

"An homage to *The Handmaid's Tale*?" suggested Ros.

"Most certainly not," declared Tessa. She hadn't read Margaret Atwood's classic for years, but Ros's question irked her. Would people think she was emulating – or worse, plagiarising, the Canadian novelist's masterpiece? The discerning reader would see at once that her style was more sophisticated than Atwood's, her sex scenes more daring; and besides, her story was really a satire on the excesses of the larger publishing houses, and the back story – about an ancient rivalry between two writers – added a most original twist. Any intelligent reader would see that.

"They say that imitation is a form of flattery," said Max, smirking.

Tessa glared at him. "Surely basing all your work on a template in which Agatha Christie meets Jeffrey Archer hardly leads to originality," she replied.

Max hefted the jug of water across the table, emptied it into his glass, and then placed it on a shelf behind him.

A slender man in black slacks and a lilac shirt entered the room and clapped his hands, demanding silence. "Welcome, everyone," he said as the chatter subsided. "My name is Marcus Dean and I am your host for this programme. Has anyone been on a Skye Creative Hub programme before?"

"*Surely* you haven't forgotten me already, Marcus?" pouted the red haired woman.

"Of course not, Pamela," said Marcus. "It's good to see you back again. Anyone else? No? Well, let me explain how we do things on these courses. But first of all, has everyone got a glass of wine?"

Murmurs and the raising of glasses assured him that they had. Only a woman in combat trousers wrapped tentative fingers around a glass of water instead.

"Then let's have a toast to you all as budding authors, and to the Skye Creative Hub, which does so much to bring out your inner bards! And let's give a warm welcome to our resident authors, Tessa Birnie and Max Logan."

The students swigged the mediocre wine and nodded in Tessa's and Max's directions in turn.

"So this is how it works," said Marcus. "We have our soup, because you'll all be hungry by now. Then we each say a little something about ourselves, just so that we can start to get to know each other. Then Megan and I will serve the main course, which tonight is prime Angus beef in red wine sauce."

"What's the vegetarian option?" asked the woman in combat trousers.

"Did you tell us you required vegetarian food?" asked Marcus.

"I stated it quite clearly on my form," said the woman.

"Oh. Well…Megan…" Marcus turned and called towards the kitchen. "Do we have a vegetarian dish tonight?"

Megan appeared at the door. "I was only expecting one vegetarian, Marcus, and that's Ms Birnie. She's got an individual tofu burger. You didn't say anything about anyone else."

"I've travelled from Bristol and my partner's paid a fortune for this course, and I'm starving," stated the woman.

"We'll sort something out, won't we Megan?" said Marcus.

"Omelette?" sighed Megan.

"I don't eat eggs," said the woman, "or wheat or dairy. As I said quite clearly on my application form."

"Let me fill up your glass," said Marcus, playing for time.

"I don't drink," said the woman.

"Can't you just eat the vegetables?" asked Pamela. "Maybe with a bit of extra bread?"

"No," said the woman.

There's always one, thought Tessa, resisting the urge to offer up her tofu burger.

"There are beans in the kitchen," said Megan. "I'll see what I can do with them."

Dee Brannigan wished she were anywhere but here. The coach journey had been long and uncomfortable and now she'd found that they hadn't read her forms properly and she wouldn't be able to eat for a week. Nuala had signed her up for the course with the best of intentions:

You've got real talent, babes, she'd said, *I'm so proud of you. Coming first in that competition is just the start. You're going places, Dee, you just need to focus on your writing. Happy birthday.*

How could Dee have disillusioned her young partner? How could she have told her what had really happened? Well, maybe this exile in the back of beyond with its plague of tiny biting insects was her punishment, and God knew, she deserved it - and worse.

Between courses, the students introduced themselves. The young woman opposite Max was Leila Morris.

"I graduated from UEA last year," she said. "Dinah Tannenbaum has just signed me up, and I'm here to spend some time finishing off my first novel."

Tessa started at the mention of her agent's name. So this was Dinah's new sensation. *She'll be the new Zadie Smith, Tessa. I don't remember when I last came across talent like hers*, Dinah had said over coffee in Starbucks, a couple of months ago. Tessa felt an instant dislike for the girl with her low cut blouse and ethnic earrings.

"I'd appreciate feedback on a couple of tricky sections, especially from you, Tessa," said Leila, although her confidence in Tessa's potential as a mentor had been somewhat lowered following a recent conversation with Dinah. *I had rather hoped she'd do better,* Dinah had mused, as they'd enjoyed dinner and a sublime bottle of Chablis at the River Café. *Her first book showed such promise, but she's been a disappointment since.* Still, thought Leila, there's that old adage, those who can, do, and those who can't, teach.

"Of course," said Tessa. "It's what we're here for."

"And I'll look forward to helping you put it to bed," said Max with a wink. All he had to do was to get Tessa out of the way.

Leon Waterson wanted the meal to be over so that he could go back to his room. His fellow students were an irrelevance, a distraction from the serious business of finishing his novel. Writing was all he wanted to do, and he doubted that either the horny old man leering at his neighbour's breasts or the woman in the linen suit with the short haircut would be a match for his talent. He'd come because his mother had paid for him to be here, and he intended to spend as much time alone with his laptop and notebooks as he possibly could. He flicked his straggly hair behind his ear as Megan plonked a soup dish in front of him. How would Major Gonzales drink soup? With grim determination, thought Leon. He'd be refuelling his body in preparation for the next battle. *And so shall I*, he decided.

"…so I couldn't have done it without the help of the British Museum," Ros was saying to Tessa. "The archive information on garden design in the seventeenth century was absolutely priceless!"

"I'm so pleased," said Tessa, hoping that she'd never have to read this woman's book.

Jack Harbottle suffered but not, alas, in silence. The trouble with his hearing aids was that they just made everything louder. Hugely and horribly louder. He felt immersed in a nightmare cacophony from which there was no easy exit. Conversation was impossible unless the person trying to converse with him had excellent and clear diction; but his fellow diners either had indecipherable regional accents or covered their mouths when they spoke or, and this was the absolute worst, spoke with their mouths full of food. The old flagstones and high ceilings and the lack of soft furnishings meant that sound amplified itself and seemed to bounce in some kind of malicious dance, choreographed to torture his ears. Of course he still would have had to come. There was no getting out of it; but how he looked forward to going back to his quiet little room in the barn conversion where his state of the art lap top awaited him, as did a bottle of eighteen year old single malt.

The best thing about being seventy-three, thought Beryl Wyndham, is that you are, to a very large extent, invisible. Too old to be seen as competition, too young to be of any antique interest. Perfect, thought Beryl.

Chapter 3

The obligatory orientation meeting saw everyone gathered in the large lounge, the students sitting expectantly with all eyes turned on Tessa and Max. The two tutors sat uneasily next to each other in ornate hardwood chairs that only added to their discomfort. Once each person had said which writer they admired most ("Well, you, Max, of course," Pamela had said, while Leila looked pensive when it came to her turn, before deciding upon Angela Carter. *Predictable,* thought Tessa. *Boring.*) The buck-toothed girl sat curled in an armchair in a shadowy corner, typing into her laptop. She'd said that her favourite author was Stephen King but had uttered nothing further. The atmosphere in the room crackled with hot tension, and everyone seemed relieved to get the meeting over with.

"Would you mind having a read of this?" Beryl asked Tessa as they headed for the door. "It's an excerpt from my novel, set in India. I'd appreciate your views."

"Of course," said Tessa, suppressing a sigh. It was sure to be some kind of romantic drivel or at best a village idyll. The worst part of these programmes was having to read the students' work, most of which, in Tessa's opinion, was dreary and banal.

After the group had dispersed, Max made his way to the reception desk. Megan wasn't there, and Max shuffled through the papers she'd left in a neat pile until he found what he was looking for. The neatly typed sheet listed participants and their room numbers. *Perfect,* thought Max.

Tessa kicked off her shoes and stretched out on her bed. She flicked open the manuscript that Beryl had handed her.

Meanwhile Lata, who was in the thickest part of the party, felt as if she was swimming in a sea of language. She was quite amazed by the glitter and glory of it all. Sometimes a half comprehensible English wave would rise, sometimes an incomprehensible Bengali one. Like magpies cackling over baubles – or discovering occasional gems and imagining them to be baubles – the excited guests chattered on.

God! How tedious, thought Tessa, relieved that Beryl hadn't given her the whole thing to read from the beginning. She wondered where she should start in giving Beryl the constructive criticism that was required on these programmes. What I ought to do, thought Tessa, is to tell her to give up hope of writing work that stands any chance of being published and take up knitting instead. But I suppose I'll just have to suggest that her work is somewhat over-written and her use of simile rather clunky. And what on earth am I to do with Max?

Max looked at his reflection in the bathroom mirror. *Not bad,* he thought, pulling the comb through his hair and arranging it so as to cover the thinning patch at the crown. He swallowed the little blue pill, gargled with minty mouthwash and then, leaving his shoes by the door, stepped into the dark hall, closing his door quietly behind him. Padding silently down the chilly corridor, he held his Zippo lighter up so as to see the numbers on the bedroom doors. Down a half flight of stairs, across a landing, up three steps, and there it was: room eleven. He could hear his heart beating in his ears and he was breathing fast. His prize was so near, and wouldn't she be pleased to see him? He pushed down on the door handle and the door gave way into the dark room. A sickly floral smell greeted him and the sound of soft snoring. He tried not to cough as he approached the bed. She was buried deep in the covers. He took off his shirt and trousers. He kicked off his boxer shorts and bent to remove his socks. Then he lifted the covers and slipped himself into the bed. The body heaved itself around and Max found himself pinioned by fleshy arms. The cloying smell made him want to gag. Surely she hadn't been wearing perfume? And surely her body was much lighter than this? Suddenly the body sat up and flicked on a bedside light.

"Max!" cried a wild-haired Pamela. "I was hoping you'd come, you naughty boy. Now just you settle down and let Pamela look after you…."

"You!" spluttered Max. "But….but…there must be a mistake…This is Leila's room."

"We swapped," said Pamela, "so that she could have the room with the shower. I prefer a bath, so it worked out perfectly. And you don't want a skinny thing like Leila, you want a real woman, Maxi. You want a woman who knows what you like…"

As she pressed her ample body to his, the perfume she'd dabbed between her breasts exploded in Max's nose and he broke into a fit of coughing.

"I can't…" he choked.

"You can!" cried Pamela

And he found, to his alarm, that the little blue pill was overriding his panic and that Pamela was right.

Pamela climaxed with a yell of triumph. Max hoped that the noise wouldn't wake everyone. He particularly hoped it wouldn't wake Tessa. He tried to get it all over and done with speedily – something that had never been a problem when he was younger, but seemed impossible now. Finally, spurred on by imagined visions of Leila's cleavage and with some adept help from Pamela, he too achieved orgasm. It was joyless and Max felt in urgent need of a shower to wash away the evidence of his humiliation and the cloying stink of Pamela's perfume.

"I have to go," he said to her. But she didn't reply. She'd curled back into sleep, a contented smile softening her face.

As he was struggling into his jeans, the door opened. The quiet girl with the protruding teeth stood there, staring at Max. He suddenly remembered where he'd met her before.

"How could you?" she whispered, and he could see that she was crying. "How could you, after what happened at Vibrant Waters? You don't even remember me, do you?"

"Ah, yes," said Max, "I knew we'd met before. Milly, isn't it? How are you?"

The girl, whose name was Anna, gave him one, last doleful look, uttered something aching and inarticulate and then turned and vanished into the dark corridor like some kind of sprite. Max could hear Pamela's contented snores begin to get louder, the interval between them growing longer as she slipped deeper and deeper into sleep. He had to get back to his room and shower off the horrible perfume residue. He hoped his chances with Leila weren't now well and truly scuppered, but he feared that they might be. He crept as quietly as he could along the corridor and slipped back into his room. Things really weren't turning out as he'd intended. First there was the unpleasantness of finding out that he was teaching with Tessa. Then there was the matter of the accommodation. And now this cock-up with the dreadful Pamela. Three things. Could this be the end of it? Would things start to look up now? Max was essentially an optimist. *It'll all start to get better tomorrow,* he thought, as he scrubbed himself under the shower. *Look on the bright side,* he said to himself: *it's not going to get worse.*

Chapter 4

The next morning, Tessa rose at 6.30, did her Pilates programme and then put on her tracksuit and trainers. There was a circular path around the extensive gardens that took her down to the little ornamental loch, along a little stream for half a mile, through some woodland and an azalea grove, and then across the lawns, back to the house. She found an early morning run helped to prepare her for the day ahead and she needed to be in good form in order to face Max Logan.

Max woke and reached for his cigarettes. *Bugger!* He thought, as he remembered the strict no smoking rules, the smoke alarm with its malevolent red wink hovering above the bed. But Max couldn't even face the shower before he'd had the first cigarette of the day, let alone talk to anyone. He pulled on yesterday's jeans and a T-shirt, took a cigarette from the pack by his bed, and headed down to the garden. He'd been dreaming about Leila Morris, and was thinking about how he could make that particular dream come true. He lit up outside the back door and inhaled deeply. Tobacco tasted infinitely better than fresh air, even air that was perfumed by heather and dewy grass. He noticed a slim figure running in the distance. He dragged on the cigarette again and the figure turned and jogged towards the house. It was Tessa, iPod clipped to her running vest, white wires leading up to her ears. *Shit,* thought Max. *I never could bear that woman first thing in the morning.* He smoked faster, the nicotine making his limbs feel liquid, his head dizzy. *I'll just finish this one,* he thought, but Tessa had reached the bottom of the lawn before he'd smoked the cigarette down to its filter. He fought against an impulse to stick out his left leg and trip her up, contenting himself with the fantasy. It was almost as satisfying as the one about bedding Leila Morris.

Tessa looked up and saw her ex-husband smoking by the back door. As she reached him, she saw the morning stubble framing his jaw, noticed that he hadn't zipped his flies. *How did I ever marry that?* She thought, remembering with distaste his whiskery morning gropings and the way he'd light a cigarette before he'd opened his eyes. In their early days together, she'd share that first smoke with him. She shuddered at the memory. Alicia Keys pumped through her headphones.

"God Max, that's revolting," Tessa panted as she reached the house. She raised her leg onto the rockery wall and stretched one hamstring, then the other. Max resisted grinding his cigarette butt into her pert behind, which somehow seemed to mock him. Instead he extinguished it in the gravel, grunted, and walked back into the house.

"Get a life, Tessa," he growled.

"And zip up your flies! You're disgusting!" called Tessa.

Max wondered if he could pull a sickie. An upstairs window closed softly.

At breakfast, Ros and Leila were deep in conversation over their muesli. Beryl buttered her brown toast and spooned on a lavish portion of apricot jam. Leon was talking with Jack, jotting notes in a spiral pad whilst listening earnestly, coffee steaming in a mug by his side. Pamela, this morning wearing a vibrant orange smock over white jeans, almost collided with Max as she carried her tray, laden with prunes and wholemeal toast towards a space at the table.

"Whoops a daisy!" she cried. "Nearly sent you flying!" Then, sotto voce, "How are you, you naughty, naughty man?"

Oh, God, thought Max. *I'm surrounded by ghastly and terrible women. This could be hell. There isn't even any bacon.* He sidestepped Pamela, muttering a barely courteous greeting, and poured himself a mug of black coffee. He had no appetite for the bowel

loosening foods on display.

"So, er, I trust you slept well?" he said to Pamela, sensing that

he had to say something more.

"Oh Maxi, that was the best night I've had in years!" said

Pamela, and he was disturbed to see that she did indeed have a certain

glow about her. "This is going to be a wonderful week!" she added,

deliberately brushing against him as she headed for a table.

Max had a frightening thought, one that chilled him so much as

to make him shudder: what if Pamela expected him to sleep with her

again?

Beryl noticed Dee sitting by herself.

"Everything all right, dear?" she asked.

"Fine," said Dee, buttering a slice of toast from the pile on the

plate in front of her. No point trying to stick to her no wheat/no dairy

routine here, she'd starve. Anyway, she wasn't sure how much good it

had done her. She'd lost a few pounds and her IBS was better, but the

truth was, she'd been more miserable than ever. "Is this your first writing retreat?" continued Beryl, interpreting Dee's gruffness as shyness.

"Yes it is," said Dee, topping the butter with a generous dollop of jam. She'd forgotten how good toast tasted.

"Have you been writing for long?" continued Beryl.

"A few months," said Dee. "How about you?"

"Oh, I'm an old hand, in more ways than one!" said Beryl.

"Published?" asked Dee, wishing the older woman would leave her alone, but sensing that she needed to try to show some interest.

"Yes," said Beryl. "I've had a little success over the years."

"That's nice for you," said Dee.

Beryl was relieved that Dee hadn't asked for details. "I'll just go and get some tea," she said, feeling that the conversation wasn't likely to go much further.

Tessa strode in bearing a glass of apple juice and a banana.

"Good morning!" she announced. "I hope you've all slept well and are ready for an intensive day. We'll meet in the seminar room in half an hour."

Unbearable, thought Max. *Utterly unbearable.*

"So Beryl," said Tessa, after the first session had ended, "you wanted some feedback."

"Yes please," said Beryl, who this morning was sporting a Paisley print blouse and elastic-waisted slacks. Not her usual style, but it was appropriate for now.

"Well, you show some promise. Watch out for over-writing and clunky metaphors."

"Thank you Tessa," said Beryl. "That's most helpful. Let me just jot that down in my notebook....Clunky metaphors, you said?"

"And over-writing."

"I see," said Beryl, wondering what the Commonwealth Foundation and millions of readers would think of Tessa's advice.

During the coffee break, Leila approached Tessa.

"Have you seen Anna today?" she asked.

Tessa had to think for a moment. Which one was Anna? Oh yes. The young woman who liked Stephen King and was in urgent need of orthodontic work.

"No," she said. "No, I don't believe I have."

Leila asked Max the same question.

"Anna?" he replied. "Which one's she?"

"You must remember," said Leila, irritated that Max couldn't remember the names of such a small group of students. "Long hair? Likes Stephen King?"

"Oh yes," said Max, "Anna. No, I can't remember seeing her since last night – since the introductory session," he hastened to add. "Yes, that's when I last saw her."

"Maybe she's gone for a walk," mused Leila. "It seems strange, though. I've asked the others – nobody has seen her this morning."

"I shouldn't worry," said Max, noting with approval that today's blouse was as casually revealing as yesterday's. "It's a shame not to go for a walk when we're in such a splendid place. How do you fancy a stroll after lunch?"

"No thank you," said Leila. "I've planned to do some editing on my novel."

"Later, perhaps?" asked Max

"Probably not," said Leila. "I prefer to walk on my own."

The more Max saw of Leila Morrison, the more he wanted her.

The more Leila saw of Max Logan, the more she loathed him. Everything she'd heard about him seemed to be true: lecherous didn't begin to describe him. And she didn't rate his writing either. If she'd have known that Sean Delancey had pulled out, she might have reconsidered coming. Surely there was some breach of the Trade Descriptions Act? In fact, it wouldn't have surprised her if Anna had packed up and gone home without bothering to say anything to either Max or Tessa. She was beginning to feel annoyed that Dinah had recommended this retreat to her: it was more than she could afford, and she'd have to work extra shifts at the arts centre to fill in the hole in her current account. Maybe she should follow Anna's example.

Leon was pleased that he'd made the effort to talk with the old man. Jack's memories of the blitz had given him an idea for a time-travelling adventure for Major Gonzales.

"The whole of London lit up like some kind of mad bonfire night," Jack was saying. "I should have been terrified, run down to the underground like everyone else, but I couldn't stop watching from the top of the hill. Jimmy Robbins and me, we just stood there watching as each explosion gave birth to a new inferno."

"Awesome," said Leon, imagining what it would be like to see schools and houses flare and buckle, all that hemmed him in destroyed, the possibilities that would emerge. "What happened to your family?"

"What's that?" asked Jack, adjusting his hearing aid.

"Your family," said Leon, louder. "What happened to them?"

"My dad was away, somewhere in France," said Jack. "Mum never made it back. She and my little sister had been at my aunt's in Balham. They went to the tube to shelter. You know the story?"

"No," said Leon.

"Station took a hit. Water pipes burst. Some people got out, lots didn't. They drowned. Water, sewage, they didn't stand a chance."

Leon felt uncomfortable. This was too much information. He'd been mapping out a scene in which Major Gonzales was beamed to London and found himself in one of those corrugated iron shelters with a sixteen year old who was gagging for it, and they had brilliant sex as London lit up around them. Thinking about it, it would make a great movie. But Jack was looking pensive, and Leon had a strange feeling in his chest, a tightening, like he might be going to cry, or something random like that.

Tessa sighed. *I'm just going to have to talk to him,* she thought. He needed to agree to her plan for the seminars and tutorials, which meant that they needed to have an adult conversation. She wasn't sure if it was possible. He was on the verandah, smoking. She'd wait until he'd finished.

Max lingered over his cigarette. Teaching this course with Tessa was going to test him to the limit. She'd been particularly spiky during the first session that morning, contradicting him at every turn, scoring points wherever she thought she could. And here she was, heading his way. He took one last drag of his cigarette before grinding out the butt under his shoe.

"I hope you're going to dispose of that properly," said Tessa.

"Oh, for fuck's sake, lighten up," said Max.

"You're so immature, Max. When are you going to grow up?"

"Get off my case, Tessa. What do you want?"

"I want to talk to you about how we're going to run this programme."

"Fine. What do you suggest?"

"Oh! That's typical! Leave all the planning to me!"

Leila watched the spatting tutors. Max was insufferable, but Tessa wasn't much better. They seemed incapable of speaking civilly to each other. It was as if they were in the middle of divorce proceedings.

Pamela heard the raised voices. She hoped that Tessa wasn't giving her Max a hard time. Maybe he needed some support.

"I'm happy to plan the course, Tessa, but you've already got it mapped out, and I lived with your control freakery long enough to know what would happen if I so much as suggested doing something different!"

"That's just a cop-out," said Tessa; but she knew that he was right. She just wanted him to agree to her plan and for the two of them to get on with teaching.

"You know I'm right," said Max.

"Fine," said Tessa. "So the next session is on developing character, ok?"

"If you say so," said Max. "But plot really needs to come first."

"No it doesn't," said Tessa. Characters make plot, not the other way round."

"No plot, no story," said Max.

"No characters, no plot," snapped Tessa.

"Now then, now then," said Pamela. "No squabbling, you two! What *are* you like?"

"Give us a moment, Pamela?" said Tessa.

Pamela winked. "It'll take more than a moment with that one!" she said, nodding towards Max.

"What's she on about?" asked Tessa.

"No idea," said Max, as Pamela shimmied towards the house. "Look, Tessa, neither of us likes this. We can find a way to work together or one of us can quit now."

"I'm certainly not quitting," said Tessa, thinking of the hole that quitting prematurely would leave in her bank account. "I owe it to these students to give them the best quality teaching I can."

"Well then, let's either toss a coin for plot or character or split the group and do half this session and half the next."

"Splitting the group's a ridiculous idea," said Tessa. "God, Max, don't you know anything about group dynamics?"

"So we'll toss," said Max, fishing a coin from his pocket. "Wanna do it?"

"Oh, for heaven's sake. I've got a splitting headache. You take the next session. I'm going for a lie down. Do what the hell you want."

She stormed back into the house, sweeping past Ros, who'd wanted to ask her about dialogue and if it should reflect the era in which it was taking place.

Plot it is, thought Max. *Round two to me.*

Tessa flung herself down on the big bed. She'd ring Zak. He'd know what to do. She reached across to her bag and fished out her iPhone. *Damn!* She looked at the little line of icons along the top. *No fucking signal! I knew I shouldn't have gone to Vodafone!* She tossed the phone across the room and closed her eyes. What would Zak say? *Just remember you're **ok**,* he'd say: *Picture your own beauty. Remember how splendid you are. Feel yourself filled with radiance.* She wished he were here. He was worth every penny of the £180 she paid per hour-long session.

Max's session on plot was going well. They'd dissected a Raymond Chandler story, and Max had asked if anyone wanted to share some of their own work.

"I'd like to think about Major Gonzales' next steps," offered Leon.

Beryl suggested that sex in an Anderson shelter might not be quite believable, especially to anyone who'd ever had to take refuge in one.

"Responding to such catastrophe by wanting sex is perfectly natural," she said, "but not in an Anderson shelter. Too much mud. Slugs, spiders, that sort of thing."

"You're quite right, Beryl," Jack had said. "Now, the neighbours' Morrison shelter was quite another matter."

"But what if the house were bombed? They could be trapped," said Ros, who thought that mixing history with science fiction was ridiculous anyway.

"What's that?" asked Jack.

"If the house was bombed, they'd be trapped," said Ros.

"It wasn't, we weren't," said Jack, winking at Beryl.

Leon decided to rethink transporting his hero into the Second World War. The court of Henry the Eighth may offer more possibilities, and he could add a beheading or two for colour. Ros would give him some tips, save him having to do all that research.

"Does Major Gonzales have to be a man?" asked Dee.

"What else could he be?" replied Leon.

"Well, women are heroic too," said Dee.

"Not in this book," said Leon.

"Sounds like a typical male wanky fantasy," muttered Dee.

"What's wrong with that?" asked Leon.

"Indeed," said Max. "Now, if we could look at what makes a good plot…"

"What's *your* book about?" Leon continued. "Lesbians in a post-apocalyptic deserted city?"

"Do you have a problem with that?"

"I don't give a shit, but Major Gonzales is a man, ok?"

Chapter 5

"Did you hear anything strange last night?" Ros asked Beryl, as they tucked into lunch.

"These old houses always creak," said Beryl. "Is that what you meant?"

"I thought I heard some rather odd noises – a woman crying, doors banging."

"Probably the wind," said Beryl, although she had thought she'd heard footsteps outside her room in the early hours.

"I expect you're right," said Ros. "It's a wonderful house, isn't it? Full of history."

"Has anyone heard from Anna?" Leila asked Tessa, after they'd finished the healthy salad that Megan had set on the table.

"I haven't," said Tessa. "She's probably gone somewhere quiet to write."

"I'm worried," said Leila. "She missed breakfast, she didn't come to either of the tutorials, and she's not come in for lunch. Shouldn't we be trying to contact her?"

"I could have a word with Marcus," said Tessa. "How are you finding Dinah Tannenbaum?"

"She's wonderful," said Leila, remembering the words of encouragement that the agent had lavished upon her at the River Café. "I find her so helpful and inspirational, don't you?"

Tessa recalled that last Starbucks coffee, when she'd had the distinct feeling that Dinah's mind was altogether elsewhere. She'd virtually timed their meeting to end after thirty minutes, saying that she had another appointment. She'd even left Tessa to pay for the coffee. "She can be useful when she thinks she can make some money from an author," she said.

"Oh, I think that's very unfair," said Leila. "She's been extremely generous with her time, and has negotiated a wonderful deal for me with Faber."

Lucky you, thought Tessa. Aloud, she said, "Well she must think your book stands a chance of selling. Have you mentioned her in your foreword?"

"Of course!" said Leila. "I've dedicated it to her."

"That would do it," muttered Tessa, ripping the skin from a satsuma.

"There's Marcus," said Leila. "I think we should talk to him about not having seen Anna."

"She'll not have gone far," said Marcus, after Leila had expressed her concerns about Anna's absence. "We're not known for our wonderful transport links here in Ardvasar! Has anyone checked her room?"

"I knocked, but no-one answered," said Leila.

"I'll ask Megan to take a look," said Marcus. "Haven't lost one yet."

Late in sitting down to lunch, Max was about to take the seat opposite Leila when Pamela called over to him.

"I've kept you a seat, Max," she called. "Come and keep me company."

Max sighed, and in the moment of hesitation, Leon took the seat opposite Leila. The only one remaining was next to Pamela. He contemplated skipping lunch, but the morning had left him hungry, so he moved across to where Pamela was patting the vacant chair.

"And how's my favourite man?" she crooned.

Dee, sitting opposite, made a grimace of disgust. As far as she was concerned, they were both revolting and probably deserved each other. But what was really occupying her was the fear that she would have to read from her work. Both Tessa and Max clearly expected students to read aloud from their writing so that they could get feedback from the others in the group. She would delay the dreadful moment for as long as she could, but this was only the first day and there were five more to go. For how long could she avoid the spotlight? They would find out just how much of a fraud she was. The only good thing was the lack of a mobile signal – she had the perfect excuse for not reporting back to Nuala on her progress.

Marcus brought an oversized dish of apple crumble to the table, but even the fragrant apple and sugar scent failed to work its usual magic for Dee.

Jack was jotting things in a little notebook, having waved away the offer of pudding.

Leila addressed the group. "Is anyone else worried about Anna?" she asked.

"Anna?" said Leon, "Should we be worried?"

"No-one's seen her since last night," said Leila. "What if she's ill, or if she's run off?"

Megan had been waiting to clear the table. "I've been meaning to check her room," she said, "but I've been busy with lunch."

"I think you should," said Leila. What was wrong with Tessa and Max, that they seemed so unconcerned about a young woman going missing?

"Please have a look, Megan," said Tessa.

Max frowned. The girl had seemed upset last night, but for the life of him, he couldn't think what he had done to distress her. She'd been on one of his Vibrant Waters programmes, but he didn't remember having had much to do with her. Maybe he'd been a little harsh with some feedback. Yes, that was probably it. He noticed that Pamela wasn't saying anything, but then she'd already been asleep when the girl had opened the door. Should he say anything? No, there wasn't any reason to confuse matters.

Half an hour later, Megan pulled Marcus into the office. "I used the master key to open Anna's bedroom door," she said, "and she's not there. The bed's made, but there are none of her things around. It looks as if she's gone. What are we to do?"

"Is there any clue to indicate where she's gone?" replied Marcus.

"I looked, but I couldn't see a note or anything. The thing is, wouldn't we have heard if she'd left? She'd have had to call a taxi at least."

"She'd have had to have called Gus's Taxis," said Marcus.

"Or maybe the other one," said Megan. "The Kyle, isn't it?"

"Christ," said Marcus. "There's always one, isn't there?"

"I think we'll need to tell Tessa and Max," said Megan. "And I'll check out the taxi firms, though I can't think how we didn't hear a car if one came."

"What about the information on her registration form?" asked Marcus. "There must be a phone number and e-mail address."

"I'll check," said Megan, glad of something positive to do.

"I'll give Tessa the news," said Marcus.

Megan longed for a quiet life. It was what had attracted her to the Skye Creative Hub in the first place. No traffic, none of the city hassle she'd struggled with for most of her life. Intermittent phone signals and primitively slow computer connections. Best of all, it was as far away from certain people as she could manage whilst still staying in the British Isles. She didn't need warring creative types and disappearing students. She unlocked her filing cabinet and extracted Anna Meredith's booking form. Anna's had been a last minute booking, and Megan hadn't checked the form as carefully as she might have done. Anna hadn't filled in the emergency contact details, and there was just one phone number for Anna's mobile. Megan dialled the number. It went straight to voicemail and invited her to leave a message.

"Hello Anna, this is Megan from the Creative Hub. I'm just calling to see if you're all right," said Megan. "We haven't seen you today. Please give me a ring."

Marcus came into the office. "Any luck?"

"No, I've left a message," said Megan

"Why do we do it, Megan?" sighed Marcus. "Why was I ever mad enough to leave Edinburgh?"

"Well, you needed to get away from…"

"It was a rhetorical question, Megan. I don't need you to remind me of …well, I just don't need to think about it." His voice had risen and Megan feared that he may be about to cry.

"I'm sorry Marcus," she said. "I didn't mean…"

"No, I know you didn't," he replied, dabbing at his nose with a linen handkerchief. "I just wish these folk would think about others from time to time."

"Writers, eh?"

"Oh, at least this lot aren't poets, Megan. Poets are the worst. You don't get worse than poets."

Chapter 6

"So, Max, we have a missing student and it's only the first day. That has to be a record," said Tessa, tapping her foot on the gravel. They were standing outside in the rose garden.

"Maybe she decided it wasn't for her," said Max. "Maybe you frightened her off."

"Me?" exclaimed Tessa. "I'm not the one who goes around leering at any woman under the age of thirty, peering down their cleavages and generally treating them like pieces of the meat you so love to gorge yourself on!"

"My, Tessa, how your grammar deserts you when you're angry," said Max. "And I hadn't looked twice at that girl. Her vanishing's got nothing to do with me."

"No, you're too busy gawping at Leila Morrison," said Tessa. "And don't think I haven't noticed you playing your little games with that ghastly woman from Croydon."

"Tessa, for someone who calls herself a writer, you're mightily unobservant," said Max. "Of course I admire Ms Morrison who, after all, is likely to be the next big thing in literary fiction. But as for Pamela, she's the one pursuing me."

"She must be pretty desperate," said Tessa.

Marcus came towards them. "Have you thought about what you want to do about Anna Meredith?" he asked.

"She hasn't returned the call?" asked Tessa.

"No, and there's no reply to the e-mail that I sent either. We checked the taxi firms, and they haven't picked up anyone from here, or anyone answering to her description."

"I suggest we give her until tonight, see if she turns up," said Max.

"And what if she's lying in a ditch dying from an overdose?" said Tessa.

In an awful moment of terrifying clarity, Max suddenly remembered his encounter with Anna at Vibrant Waters. *Oh no!* he groaned to himself.

"Max?" asked Tessa.

"Nothing," said Max.

"But you've turned quite pale, hasn't he Marcus?"

"You do look a little peaky," Marcus agreed.

Max reached into his pocket for a cigarette. His hand trembled as he tried to light it.

"Do you have to?" asked Tessa

"Fuck off, Tessa," snapped Max. "Just fuck off and leave me alone."

"Don't you dare talk to me like that!" said Tessa. Nevertheless, she took a step backwards, away from the smoke and Max's anger. "I suppose I'll have to take this afternoon's tutorial."

"That would be for the best," said Marcus, who'd been standing on the sidelines, but was getting increasingly concerned about the poisonous atmosphere being created by Tessa and Max. It wasn't what the Skye Creative Hub was all about. It just wouldn't do. But how could he get things back to some kind of harmonious normality?

"What's it got to do with you, Marcus?" barked Max, lighting another cigarette.

"I run this centre, Mr Logan," said Marcus. "May I remind you that we have a reputation to uphold, customers who have paid good money to come somewhere to explore their creativity."

"I'll take the tutorial, Max," said Tessa. "Go and chill. You can take the session before supper."

"I've got Leon's extract to read," said Max. "I'll use the time to do that. Probably go to sleep." He sounded gruff, but something approaching kindness coming from Tessa had softened his temper.

Thank God! Thought Tessa, as Max headed for his room. *I'll teach the group for a short session, then set them a task that they can work on individually so that I can do some work on my novel. I think I'll review the scene in the maternity ward.*

"So, Leila, what can you tell us about the characters you're currently writing?"

"The central character is called Fen, who's in a relationship with Monk. They've been through a major crisis and they go back a long way, but now Fen wants to break free. When Tree takes a job in the design company where Fen works, Fen's torn between desire for Tree and loyalty to Monk."

"Thank you Leila," said Tessa. "Please read us a passage so that we can see how you build your characters."

"Ok," said Leila. *"Fen pressed the go button on the photocopier and watched the paper feed through, only to be spewed back by the machine. Like my life, Fen thought. I always end up back in the same place. The iPhone in Fen's pocket vibrated. A message had come through. It was from Monk. When Fen opened it, there was nothing there. Was Monk saying something profound, or was the empty space simply the result of the keypad not being locked? Fen grabbed the papers and took them back to the large table around which they all worked. Tree was working on an intricate graphic. Fen watched the fine movement of Tree's long, delicate hand and ached with desire. If only each person had more than one life, if only we really were living an infinite number of lives simultaneously. If only Fen could take Tree by the hand, by the lovely hand, and lead them both to somewhere soft and quiet where they could explore, could discover each other, without hurting Monk, without changing what had been constant for so long.*

"Fen, come look at this," said Tree. "I'm feeling that the text should be fourteen point, what do you think?""

Tessa could not believe that Dinah was willing to lavish time and money on such paltry talent. Still, she wouldn't say anything. She'd leave it to the other group members.

"Thoughts, anyone?" she said

There was a long silence before Pamela said, "These people, Leila, why have they got such funny names?"

"They've got the names they came with," said Leila. "I didn't consciously think of them, they just sort of came – I got the vision of the person and they were speaking their name. Does that sound crazy?"

"It does a bit," said Pamela.

"It's not just the funny names, but I can't tell which are the boys and which the girls," said Jack. "Or maybe I just didn't catch everything."

"The ambiguity is deliberate," said Leila.

Poser, thought Tessa.

"So they could be men fancying men, or women fancying women?" said Dee, looking interested for the first time since they'd all arrived.

"Or one man and two women or two women and one man," said Leila.

"But you must know, in your mind, what each character is?" said Ros.

"Or are they androgynous aliens?" asked Leon.

"It's for the reader to work out," said Leila. "The story is what you think it is. There are no absolute truths."

"Does Leila's style work?" asked Tessa, hoping to be provocative.

"Not for me," said Ros. "Sorry Leila, but I think these people are more like ciphers that real characters. I don't feel for them."

"I think it's brilliant that you've taken gender out of the story," said Dee.

"I don't think they'd be using a photocopier," said Leon.

"I wouldn't want to think there'd be buggery later on," said Jack, wanting to be provocative.

"Thank you," said Leila. "That's all really helpful."

Well that's my bit over and done with, she thought. *With any luck I won't have to read any more and can just get on with finishing the writing. Who on earth do they think they are, anyway?*

Beryl was the only one who hadn't said anything. Now she thought that it would be polite to say something.

"I liked the image of the paper in the machine," she said, "I thought that worked very well. The analogy between the machine and Fen's life. I think you could build on that."

"Thank you," said Leila, thinking that this was the most sensible comment she'd heard. "I'll play with it and see what happens."

Next Ros read from her historical novel. She read at a rapid pace, and it was difficult for the group to take in the words. Still, the response was warm, with people saying that they really felt themselves in the seventeenth century with her heroine, especially when she described the sanitary arrangements.

"I think we'll break for the rest of the afternoon," said Tessa. "I'd like you each to go and do some work on one of your characters, and be prepared to talk about them in the session tomorrow. I want us to feel that your character is so real, that he or she has a place at this table. They should walk, talk, breathe, eat, shit, sleep, sing – in tune or out of tune – and we need to know all about them."

There was a murmur as people jotted down the task in their notebooks or on their laptops, and then the group dispersed.

Tessa headed for her lovely bedroom and thought about the next steps she wanted to take with her novel, a piece of literature so superior to anything she'd heard this afternoon that it was if people from different planets were attempting to do the same kind of thing but with those from the student planet having neither the creative spark nor the wordsmith skills to produce real literary art.

Beryl found a bench in the shade in the rose garden. She breathed in the scent of the blooms and allowed herself to bask in the sultriness of the afternoon. If only she wasn't here to…no, she wouldn't think about it. She'd take a few moments to enjoy the beauty of the place and set aside the rest. There were, after all, five more days to go. And then…no, she wouldn't think about that just now.

Jack poured a whisky and turned on his laptop. The story was taking shape nicely, and he wasn't short of material. He was struggling to hear, that was for sure, but his deafness had made him more observant, he'd noticed. The deafer he became, the more he watched.

And he'd been told that his more mature works were significantly better observed than his earlier ones. Some of that could be attributed to age: once one lost the urgency of youth, one was able to relinquish a certain amount of self-absorption, he'd found. Jack wondered if he'd ever been as callow as Leon. Beryl seemed nice, but she was something of a dark horse. He'd try to get to know her better. Maybe they could sit together at dinnertime. He wondered what had happened to the girl who seemed to have gone missing. Anna, they called her. He'd noticed her looking in a queer sort of way at Max Logan, and he'd tried to fathom what the look could mean. There was something furtive and also injured about it. Maybe Logan had been critical of the girl's writing, although she'd disappeared before the first tutorial, and he hadn't noticed her giving the tutor anything to read. Well, she'd either turn up or she wouldn't. It was all grist to his own mill, so he opened up his laptop and set to work.

Pamela and Ros had decided to go for a walk.

"These midges'll be the death of me," said Pamela, swotting at the miniature menaces in vain.

"I find citronella helps," said Ros. "Of course the Elizabethans knew how to keep insects and pests away," she added. "They wouldn't be without potions containing rue, tansy, or lavender."

"You're very knowledgeable about the Elizabethan period," said Pamela, feeling somewhat in awe of Ros and her encyclopaedic brain.

"As a novelist, I find I spend more time on the research than on the writing. It's so vital to get the details right and to conjure the era with care."

"Yes, I suppose so," said Pamela. "I spent a lot of time in the Whitgift Centre in Croydon researching my book. And of course I made sure that my description of the Fairfield Halls car park was accurate – that was a bit dodgy, to tell you the truth, all piss and concrete."

"Charming," murmured Ros.

"Well, I say, tell it how it is," said Pamela, "and that car park has seen more pee than the gents' at Waterloo Station."

"So what's your book about?" asked Ros.

"A serial killer on the loose in Croydon," said Pamela. "He stalks women shoppers and strangles them in car parks. Daisy

Honeyman is the private eye who goes on the trail of the murderer and finally catches up with him."

"Why Croydon?" asked Ros, thinking that her research outings to Hampton Court sounded much more savoury.

"Local colour," said Pamela. "Or lack of it. All that grey concrete, and dear Max had shown how much could be done with a shopping centre in *Blood in the Mall*."

"I see," said Ros, thinking that it took all sorts.

"How about you?" asked Pamela, "What are you working on?"

"A family saga set in the seventeenth century around a theme of garden design. You've heard of Tradescant?"

"I'm afraid you've got me there!" said Pamela. "Who's he?"

"Tradescant is probably the best known gardener and collector of plants in the sixteenth and seventeenth centuries. He was Head Gardener to the Earl of Salisbury at Hatfield House." She gave a little sniff. She was proud of her knowledge of characters from history.

"Sounds fascinating," said Pamela, thinking that she'd probably be bored before she reached the end of page one of Ros's book.

The two women had left the grounds of the Creative Hub and were walking along the quiet lane that led to the village, which was a mile away.

"Shall we go into the village and investigate the pub?" asked Pamela.

"We've a couple of hours to go before dinner," said Ros, "It'd be nice; but we have to produce that character sketch for Tessa's next tutorial."

"Plenty of time for that," said Pamela. "We could jot down some notes over a nice glass of wine."

They carried on towards the little village of Ardvasar.

"My feet are killing me!" sighed Pamela. "Let's find somewhere to sit down."

The Ardvasar Hotel was open, so they went in and ordered a glass of wine each, and then settled at a table in a quiet corner. The bar was almost deserted. A man who could have been a fisherman sat at the counter and sipped from a pint of amber coloured beer. A young couple in walking gear played Scrabble at another table.

"Ye'll be at the Creative Hub, then?" said the barman as he placed their glasses on the table.

"Yes," said Ros. "We're there for the best part of the week."

"You're in luck: it's not forecast to rain for a couple of days," said the man.

Lovely accent, thought Pamela. *Such a handsome face. A bit like Denis Lawson.*

"One of your crowd was in here earlier," he continued.

"Oh?" said Ros, expecting him to describe Max Logan.

"Quiet wee lassie," he said. "Think she'd really just come in to use the toilet, but had an orange juice to make it less obvious."

"What did she look like?" asked Pamela.

"I didnae take much notice," said the barman. "Young, long hair, you know the type. Why, have you lost one?" He chuckled, but Pamela and Ros were looking at each other.

"Yes," said Ros. "As a matter of fact, we have."

Chapter 7

The possible sighting of Anna had excited Ros and Pamela, and they walked briskly back to the Creative Centre.

"We need to let them know as soon as possible," said Pamela, relishing the thought of being the bearer of interesting news.

The other students were already gathering for dinner. Marcus and Megan were bustling around with platters and the smell of something savoury was enticing.

"Excuse me," shouted Pamela, clapping her hands, "Can we please have your attention?" The buzz of conversation continued. "EXCUSE ME!" Everyone turned to look at the two women.

"We've got some news about Anna," said Pamela.

"Well, we think we may *possibly* have some news about Anna," said Ros.

"We went to the local pub, and the landlord said a young woman had been in earlier. It sounded as if it could have been Anna."

"Are you sure?" asked Marcus. "Did he give a good enough description?"

"He said she was quiet and had long hair," said Pamela.

"But that could have been anyone," said Tessa.

"What made him think she had come from here?" asked Megan.

"We asked him that, and he said he could just tell," said Ros. "Something about looking pale and having ink stains on her chin. Not wearing hiking boots."

"Well, that's good, isn't it?" said Max.

"Only in as much as it suggests she's not lying dead in a ditch," said Leila. "We don't know where she is now, or why she left."

Max didn't say anything. He thought he knew why the girl left.

"I still think we should let the police know," said Megan.

"I'll have a word tomorrow," said Marcus. "Now, everyone, let's eat."

Dee was beginning to think she'd turn into a baked bean. But at least there were some fresh vegetables and the beans were encased in a large, buttery jacket potato. And she'd seen Megan making a blackberry crumble for pudding. She wouldn't starve. She'd struggled to do the task that Tessa had set the group. Her characters always seemed so lifeless; but sitting in her room, just writing and writing, she'd suddenly found that Lou, her protagonist, was taking on a life of her own. She felt that here was someone she could sit down with and have a conversation. Someone she'd like to have as a friend. She'd go and do some more work after dinner. She wanted to tell Nuala, but there was still no phone signal. She'd ask Megan if she could use the office computer to send an e-mail later on. Those in the students' computer room had to have the slowest internet connection in the world. Of course Nuala would see nothing remarkable in Dee creating a lifelike character. Nuala believed that Dee's writing was original, getting on for brilliant. After all, she'd been a runner-up in a major international competition, and her story was there in print in that book of winning stories. Maybe, Dee thought, there was a kind of redemption happening. Maybe God, not the patriarchal one of course, more like Goddess, had decided to give her a break. Maybe Nuala needn't find out she was a fraud. She thought about that nun at school, the one who taught English, the one who hated her. Sister Immaculata. *You know what, Sister? You can go fuck yourself.* For the first time since arriving at the Skye Creative Hub, Dee smiled.

Leon was having trouble with Major Gonzales. He'd had a vivid dream the previous night, and it had disturbed him greatly. In it, Major Gonzales had stripped off his uniform in the middle of the space station only to reveal that he was, in fact, a woman. Every time Leon tried to write the next stage in the saga, his character seemed to be giving him bizarre messages. Attempting Tessa's homework, he started to describe the Major by showing what was in his pockets. Laser lance, spun steel cord, communication box: those were all perfectly normal; but then Leon found himself writing tampon, lip balm, nail file. And to make things worse, when he abandoned the character sketch and went back to the plot, instead of knocking his rival unconscious as each battled to lead the mission, he found himself writing them sitting in a soft-hued room, talking over their differences with a mediator. It was totally unbelievable, but Leon seemed quite unable to get his story back on track.

Tessa grimaced as she saw Max approaching.

"Anything I need to know about tomorrow?" asked Max.

"I thought we'd get them developing their characters and critiquing each others' work," said Tessa. "Any objections?"

"I rather had in mind a session on driving the plot forward," said Max.

"After lunch," said Tessa.

"The graveyard shift," said Max. "They'll be stuffed full of food and half asleep. I say we start with plot, get them to talk about pace."

"They need to move on with what we started today," said Tessa. "You can lead the afternoon session. I'm sure you'll be able to keep them awake and alert."

"Whatever," said Max. "What about the missing girl? D'you think she caught the first ferry out? Realised she'd made a mistake?"

"Maybe. The sighting in the village suggests she's alive and well. I don't think there's much more we can do. It's not as if she was here long enough for anyone to have upset her."

"Of course not," agreed Max.

"Good God, Max, you're actually agreeing with me about something?"

"I shouldn't get too excited about it," grunted Max; but he was relieved that Tessa was as keen as he was to put Anna's appearance and disappearance behind her.

Jack sat next to Beryl at the dinner table. She seemed to welcome him, shifting along the bench to make room.

"How's it going?" she asked, passing him a dish of new potatoes.

"Coming along," said Jack, "Slowly, though. I could do with a day just to write."

"What's your book about?" asked Beryl. "You've been very quiet. You haven't really said anything yet."

"I don't think they've noticed, do you?" asked Jack, his eyes twinkling.

"I think they're rather too absorbed in trying to outdo each other," said Beryl.

"And we're too old to bother about," said Jack. "It's rather liberating, don't you think?"

Beryl smiled, and passed him a bowl of carrots.

"Anyway, Beryl," Jack said, "it's not as if we've heard much from you either!"

"I did give a piece to Tessa last night," said Beryl, "and she gave me a brief critique. But you haven't answered my question, Jack: what's your book about?"

"Eh?" said Jack, adjusting his hearing aid.

"Don't play the deaf card!" laughed Beryl. "You heard! The subject of your book!"

"I'll tell you, but you're not to mention anything to anyone else," said Jack. "If you do, it'll spoil everything."

"Now I'm intrigued!" said Beryl. "Tell me more, please do."

"You've read my other books?" asked Jack in a whisper, leaning closer to Beryl .

"I don't know that I have," said Beryl, surprised to find that he was published: he'd presented himself as something of a novice.

"I write under another name," he said. "You may know me as…"

But at that moment, the lights went out, and the room was enveloped in darkness.

"What's happening?"

"Who switched the lights off?"

"Ha, ha, joke's over, put the lights on!"

"Ouch! That's hot!"

"Keep calm everyone," called Marcus, above the din. "It's just a power cut. I'll try to find some candles. Anyone got a torch?"

The sound of people panicking rose to a cacophony. There was a crash as crockery was knocked from the table.

"You forget how dark the countryside is," said Beryl.

"Like the blackout," said Jack.

Marcus had been standing near the door. He felt his way into the kitchen and groped blindly towards the drawer where he knew the emergency supplies were stored. Pulling it open, he moved his hand gingerly, feeling for the candles. His fingers found a small box. Matches, a good start. He explored further, and found something small, stubby, waxy. He pulled it out and felt for the wick. Sliding the matchbox open, he took out a match and struck it on the side. Nothing happened. He tried another, and the same thing happened. The box was dry, but the matches must all be spent. Why did people feel the need to put dead matches back in the matchbox? He stumbled back into the dining room, clutching the stub of candle.

"Anyone got a lighter?" he asked, trying to remember if anyone in this group smoked.

"I have," said a man's voice.

Marcus edged towards the voice, which he'd recognised as belonging to Max.

"Watch where you're going!" cried a woman, whose chair Marcus had knocked.

"I'm doing my best!" cried Marcus. God! These people could be so self-centred. "Where are you, Max?"

"Here," said Max, sounding close by.

"Use your lighter," said Marcus.

Max flipped open his Zippo and an eerie light seeped into the gloom. Marcus held out the candle.

"Light this," he said to Max.

The little candle threw faint light around the table. Faces looked ghastly, frightened.

"Lend me your lighter, and I'll see if I can find more," said Marcus. Max handed over the Zippo, and Marcus retreated to the kitchen. The panic had subsided and now there was a sense of simmering fear in the room. Marcus went back to the drawer and used Max's lighter to peer deeper and try to find the candles. There'd been a box of six last time he'd looked. Now there was nothing of any use. A corkscrew, a first aid box, a pair of scissors, a ball of string. No candles. These power cuts normally lasted a few minutes at most. He reckoned it had been five at least since the lights went out. What on earth was he to do?

Chapter 8

Leon didn't have to think to hard to figure out what Major Gonzales would do in a situation like this. He'd take care of the vulnerable and frightened, shoot down the looters, and then find the source of the power cut, before restoring the flow of electricity, which would lead to a return to light, calm, and order. He listened to the sounds around him. It didn't sound as if there was much looting going on. He reached across to Leila.

"Don't worry, it'll be all right," he said.

"Oi! Get your hands off!" Leila yelled back.

"S-s-sorry," stammered Leon, "I meant to touch your arm. I can't see."

"None of us can bloody well see," said Leila.

"I just wanted to reassure you that it'd be all right and I'm here to watch out for you," said Leon.

"Who says gallantry is dead?" said Leila, and Leon didn't need light to know that there was a hard little smirk on her face. "Hey, Leon, this may be news to you, but we women know how to take care of ourselves."

"He was just trying to be nice," said Ros.

"I know," sighed Leila. "Look, Leon, I'm sorry, ok? It's just that this week is turning out to be a complete nightmare."

"I don't know why everyone's so glum," exclaimed Pamela. "This is fun! We could play murder in the dark."

Assorted groans greeted this suggestion. Someone muttered *someone should murder her* but Pamela couldn't tell who had uttered this unkind response to her trying to lighten the atmosphere.

Marcus remembered finding the corkscrew. "I'll try to find us some wine," he said. "Can I borrow your lighter again, Max?"

Max passed him the Zippo, and Marcus trod a careful path back to the kitchen. He fumbled in the wine rack, which was near the door, and took out two bottles – never mind the colour or vintage, this was an emergency. Flipping down the top of the lighter, which was becoming too hot to handle, he reached into the drawer, feeling for the corkscrew. It wasn't there. He groped around some more, but there was nothing that felt anything like a corkscrew. He was sure it had been there before.

"Sorry folks," he said, edging back into the dining room. "Corkscrew's gone AWOL."

"No screw tops?" Max asked, trying to sound hopeful.

"'Fraid not," said Marcus.

"Where's the fuse-box?" asked Dee. "Maybe one of the fuses has just tripped."

"Under the stairs," said Megan. "I don't think we could find it in the dark."

"I'll help you try," offered Dee.

"I'll come too," said Leon, knowing that this would be Major Gonzales' response, and somewhat peeved that he hadn't thought of it before Dee.

The little candle guttered and died, plunging the room, once more, into total blackness.

"I don't know…" said Megan, who was afraid of the dark. This house that she'd begun to call home suddenly seemed eerie, as if its shadow side had revealed itself in a fit of anger.

"Come on," said Dee, surprising herself at her bravery, but sensing that her heroine, Lou, would do the same. "Otherwise we'll be waiting around here until dawn."

"I'll come with you," said Leon.

Three shadows crept their way towards the door to the hall, inching along the wall, holding hands to ensure they stayed together.

Pamela was aware of Max's warm body next to hers. Quietly, slowly, she reached her hand across to him. She started to stroke his leg. It was wonderful that no-one could see. The darkness was liberating. Max reached down and grabbed Pamela's hand, moving it back firmly to her own lap. Pamela stretched her other arm over and took hold of Max's hand before it could find its way home. Max pulled away, appalled at where her hand was leading his; but Pamela was strong and tugged back.

"Stop it, Pamela," whispered Max, thankful that no-one could see what was happening.

"Oh, go on, Maxi," cooed Pamela. "I'm all nice and ready for you."

"No!" shouted Max. The violence of his movement as he yanked his arm back caused him to lurch to the other side and all of a sudden he was falling, his chair toppling on top of him. At the point where he hit the floor, the room was dazzlingly flooded with light.

"We did it!" cried Leon, skipping, then striding back into the room. Major Gonzales wouldn't ever skip, he'd stride, manfully.

Dee followed, a satisfied grin lighting her face. Megan was close behind, looking relieved and feeling proud that she'd faced her fear and saved the day.

There was applause from everyone, except Max, whose back had twisted in his fall. Spasms of pain arced through his body as he tried hard not to cry out loud.

"What on earth are you doing on the floor?" Tessa asked Max.

"What's it look like?" Max gasped, each breath proving to be agonising.

Pamela looked on in dismay.

"Come on, don't be such a wimp," said Tessa

"I think he's really hurt," said Megan, crouching down, and fighting her instinctive distaste for the man. "Mr Logan, should I call an ambulance?"

"Don't be ridiculous," said Tessa. "Come on Max, you've had your attention, now stop being stupid. We've got the evening tutorial to run."

If Max had had a gun at that point, he would have shot Tessa between the eyes, shot her dead. But he didn't have a gun, or any other kind of weapon. He tried to stretch a leg, but every move made him want to scream.

"Try breathing deeply," said Ros, who was a great believer in natural remedies. "You need to release the tension."

"I could help," said Pamela. "How about I rub your legs? Maybe your neck?"

"I think you've done enough for one night," said Max.

"The strange thing is," said Dee, "that the mains switch was off. It wasn't a single fuse that had tripped, they were all in order. It's as if someone had turned the power off deliberately."

"Who would have done that?" said Beryl, the only one to be taking any notice of Dee.

"We were all here," said Dee. "And it would have to have been someone who knew where the fuse box was."

"It's in the cupboard where we put our outdoor clothes," said Leon, joining the conversation. "I'd noticed it when I hung my jacket up. Anyone observant would have noticed. And we're all supposed to be writers, people good at watching and noticing."

Marcus approached the little group. "Thank you," he said. "You've done well. Which fuse had tripped?"

Dee explained about the mains switch.

"Was it you, Marcus?" asked Beryl. "Was this a little exercise in group survival?"

Marcus laughed. "I'd have timed it to have happened at a much more convenient time – like just when I wanted you all to go to bed and leave me in peace to clear up!"

But Marcus was troubled: what had happened to the box of candles? How come there was a corkscrew in the drawer when he went to it the first time, and then a few minutes later, it had gone? And who had the opportunity, let alone the volition, to switch the power off, bringing disturbance to the household?

"Marcus, I think we need to call an ambulance for Mr Logan," said Megan. "He can't move."

"You think we'll get one at this time of night, out here?" snorted Marcus.

"We could ask Dr Mackintosh to come and take a look," said Megan.

"Just get me some help," groaned Max. "Please," he added, with a sob.

Chapter 9

Dr Mackintosh was not a happy man. He'd been enjoying a venison dinner with his good friend Archie MacLure, and he oughtn't to have been driving. He didn't approve of the Skye Creative Hub. It attracted all sorts of weird folk. He recalled one time when he'd been called out three times in the same week to administer to a lassie who wasn't right in the head. Hysterical, they used to call it, only you weren't supposed to call it that these days. Too much poetry, that was the problem. They were a crabbit lot, and he was none too pleased himself after the third trek out to the centre. Poets! Hard work was what they needed. Hard, manual labour.

So here he was again, dragging himself up the steep drive. Wee Megan Kennedy opened the door to him and showed him to the patient.

A middle aged man lay awkwardly on the floor. Dr Mackintosh could tell straight away that he was in pain: his face was grey, and his breathing shallow. The crowd around him displayed a range of reactions: a woman who, in Dr Mackintosh's opinion, needed putting on a medically supervised diet, stood anxiously near the patient's feet, chubby hands flapping uselessly at her side, her round face creased in concern. The patient seemed to be cringing away from her. Then there was the smart, slim woman, standing to one side, hands on hips like some no-nonsense matron. A chunky woman with spiky hair was cleaning her short nails with a paperclip. An elderly man appeared to be dozing in the far corner. Everyone else either chatted quietly or sat at the table looking exhausted.

"Give me some room," ordered Dr Mackintosh, as he bent to examine Max.

"Where's it hurting?" he asked.

Max indicated as best he could where the spasm had its epicentre.

"Oh aye," said the doctor feeling under Max's shirt. "We'll soon have you moving. Nothing broken."

"Shouldn't he have an x-ray?" asked Pamela

"Let's try this first," said Dr Mackintosh, drawing fluid into a capacious syringe.

"What is it?" asked Max, wondering how much worse this day could get. He had a horror of needles, and this one looked long enough to go right through him.

"Valium," said Dr Mackintosh. "You'll feel lovely all over."

"Aggh!" shrieked Max, as the doctor plunged the needle into his back.

Dr Mackintosh released the drug slowly into Max's body.

"Haven't you finished yet?" cried Max.

"Can't rush this," said Dr Mackintosh, "or you could end up in a very nasty way."

"I *am* in a very nasty way!"

"I do know what's best," said the doctor, wondering if this one was a poet too. At last, having pushed the plunger all the way down, he pulled out the needle. "There, all done," he said. "As soon as you can, get yourself more comfortable, and then if one or two of these kind folk would help you, I'd suggest you go straight to bed. I'll leave some tablets for you. Take two now."

Megan brought him a glass of water, and Max swallowed the pills. He soon felt his muscle relax, as if by magic.

"Thank you, doctor," he said. He was overcome by a heavy drowsiness. He tried to move his legs. It didn't hurt, not much, anyway.

"Let me help you upstairs," said Major Gonzales, via Leon.

"I'll help too," said Pamela, eager to be of use.

"No Pamela," said Max, more sharply than he'd intended, "I'll be fine with Leon."

"Oh," said Pamela, looking as deflated as it was possible for a woman in an Evans smock to look. "Oh. Well, you know where I am if you need anything…" Maybe he'd be in need of comfort a little later in the evening.

"I won't," said Max. "Goodnight Pamela. Why don't you write something?"

Max opened the door to his room, and Leon reached to switch on the light.

"Wow!" said Leon. "I thought I was messy! This is something else."

Max shuffled in and groaned, as he took in the dreadful sight that met his eyes. Someone had ransacked his room, turning out his drawers, stripping the linen from his bed and tossing it around the room. There was a smell of mint, and as he looked closer, he saw that his clothes were striped with toothpaste. Staggering into the bathroom, he saw with dismay that his medicine bottles had been emptied and now lay on the floor, their contents who knew where. Shaving foam dripped down the mirror, the empty can discarded in the sink. Max reached into his pocket for a cigarette. Bugger the rules. The packet was empty, so he went to get a new one from his bedside table. To his horror, all five packets had been opened, and their contents cut into pieces small as dolly mixtures. "Fuck!" said Max. "What the fuck's going on?"

"Someone doesn't like you?" suggested Leon.

"Tessa! It's got to be fucking Tessa!" cried Max. "Wait 'til I get my hands on that tight arsed bitch…"

"It might not be her," said Leon.

"Oh, it is, trust me," said Max. "That's it. I've had it with her. She wants a fight, she's fucking got a fight!" And he turned, determined to hunt out his ex-wife and punish her for this desecration; but the valium and sedatives were reaching the peak of their potency, and he found he couldn't take another step. As he faltered, Major Gonzales stepped in to prevent his falling. He helped Max to the bed, eased him onto the mattress, and took off his shoes. He shook out the duvet and covered Max with it, taking care to put the least minty part nearest his head. Before he'd finished, Max was deeply unconscious and snoring.

Major Gonzales, for Leon now felt himself to be fully in character, closed Max's door and went back downstairs. Marcus and Megan were clearing the table of the debris left from dinner. Tessa had taken the students into the sitting room to start the evening tutorial. Gonzales strode into the centre of the room and pointed at Tessa.

"How do you account for your actions this evening, Ms Birnie?"

"I beg your pardon, Leon?"

"Desecrating Mr Logan's room. Why did you do it?"

"I haven't desecrated anyone's room, and I wouldn't go near Max's if you paid me. What's happened?"

Everyone was now looking at Leon. Major Gonzales faded into the background, and Leon answered, "Mr Logan's room was turned over. It's a total mess."

"Was he robbed?" asked Beryl, who thought that this course was getting more interesting by the minute.

"I don't know," said Leon. "It looked more vindictive than anything. I suppose we'll have to ask him in the morning – he was about to come after Ms Birnie, but he crashed out. Meds kicked in."

"Who would have done it? We were all in the dining room this evening," said Leila.

"Some people left the room," said Ros, pointedly, looking at Dee.

"Yeah, right," said Dee. "Megan, Leon and me. We went to sort out the fuse, and then came straight back. Are you trying to suggest something?"

"I'm simply saying that you three left the room," said Ros. "No-one else did."

"And if one of us had snuck upstairs to tear up Max's room, the others would have noticed," said Leon, indignant at Ros's insinuation.

"Anyway, what'd be the point?" asked Dee. The last thing she'd think about doing was going into some bloke's room. You never knew what you might find.

"Could Marcus have anything to do with it? I mean, he'd know where the power switch was, too," said Leila.

"Why would he?" asked Tessa. "He's got the most to lose: he needs this centre to work, he needs us to recommend it to others."

Jack wished he could hear what everyone was saying. It was so frustrating. He gathered that Max had gone to bed, that something was amiss upstairs, and that people were almost, but not quite, arguing. He got up and moved closer to Beryl.

"Any idea what's going on?" he asked.

"Someone's vandalised Max Logan's room," said Beryl.

"Not surprised," said Jack.

"Why?"

"He's pissed off half the group one way or another."

"I know that he and Tessa are like cat and dog," said Beryl. "What else have you noticed?"

"That woman in orange is all over him like a rash, and he doesn't like her one bit," said Jack. "Definitely giving her the brush-off. Hell hath no fury, and all that."

"How observant!" said Beryl.

"And then there's that pretty young thing with the earrings, what's her name?"

"Leila?"

"That's the one. Well he can't keep his eyes off her breasts. Haven't you noticed the glares she's throwing at him?"

"Well, yes, now you mention it. And she did say something about it yesterday."

"And I don't think he's managed to charm the historian or the dyke, do you?"

"Jack!" exclaimed Beryl.

"Well, I can't hear their names. They all mumble too much. And if I do hear, I don't remember."

Beryl laughed. Jack may not have got the hang of political correctness, but he was funny, and she liked his acute powers of observation. And hadn't he been telling her about the books he'd written just before the lights went out? She wondered if she dared to share her secret with him. Better not. Not just yet.

Marcus and Megan were putting away the dishes.

"I'm worried, I'll not deny it," said Marcus. "All these strange happenings. It can't all be a coincidence."

"You think not?" said Megan, who was getting increasingly nervous.

"Well you tell me, Megan. Who switched the power off? If it wasn't you or me, who was it? Who knew where the switch was?"

"Well, anyone hanging up their coat could have…"

"Yes, I know that if they were observant enough they'd have seen it; but why? What would anyone get out of it?"

"A good story?"

"You may have something there," said Marcus, stroking his chin. "I hadn't thought of that. But wouldn't we have seen someone leave the dining room?"

"I'd have thought so, but maybe they snuck out and back in again really quietly. Maybe they were furtive," she added, liking the sound of the word.

"I can't see any of that lot being quiet and furtive," said Marcus. Especially not that Pamela woman. Not Dee, either. Leon's a slight sort of bloke, but he was at the wrong end of the room. Leila? The budding prize-winner?"

"She seems too strait-laced, and she was genuinely peeved," said Megan. "At least, I think she was."

"I can't see Ros doing it," said Marcus.

"No, definitely not Ros. That leaves the oldies."

"They couldn't move quickly enough. Wouldn't they knock things over?"

"I don't know, they're pretty fit for their age, Beryl especially."

"Are we ruling out Tessa?"

"She's too busy with her book and trying to outdo Max. Anyway, why would she? She needs this week to work so that we book her again."

"You know what else is bothering me?" said Marcus.

"Max's room?"

"No, apart from that. Of course that bothers me, but I think it's most likely to have been Tessa Birnie. No, it's the candles going missing, and the corkscrew that was there, only then it wasn't."

"D'you think we have a poltergeist?"

"I'm beginning to wonder."

Chapter 10

Tessa was reviewing the students' progress in character development. Ros had read an extract from her ongoing novel. Tessa found it dreary beyond measure: Ros had described the garden with encyclopaedic detail, but her characters' dialogue was stilted and she'd attempted to use speech of the time. When she read it out loud it was as if Pepys had time-travelled to Walton on Thames. Tessa could see Dee and Leon trying hard to suppress giggles.

"Try to make the speech flow more naturally," she said, mustering as much diplomacy as she could, given the dramas of the day and evening. "And maybe offer the occasional suggestion of the dialogue of the era, rather than trying to translate all of your speech," she added. "Now, who else is going to read? Dee, we haven't heard from you, yet."

It was the moment that Dee had been dreading, but strangely, since the incident with the fuse box, she felt braver and more confident. People might even like what she'd written. *Yeah, and pigs might sprout wings,* she said to herself.

"Here goes, then," she said, clearing her throat. "*Lou sat down on a park bench and opened her bag. She took out the sandwich and sighed. It looked as sad as she felt, its edges curling up as if dying, the miserable little portion of cheese inside shiny and dry, the margarine*

rancid. My life's like that sandwich, thought Lou. Once, it had been

fresh. I should have eaten it when I bought it, not left it lying around

for a day before remembering it was there, she thought. Her appetite

gone, she chucked the sandwich into the nearest bin. She still had to

decide what to do about Marcia. Four weeks with no word. What did

that mean? Lou thought it probably meant that Marcia was bored with

her and couldn't be bothered to phone or write or arrange to meet up.

Lou had that effect on people. Lou always thought it was her fault.

Anything. Whatever was going wrong was her fault. The worldwide

recession probably had something to do with her – or at least, that's

what she thought when she was at her bleakest. But what if there was

something else going on with Marcia that had nothing to do with her?

What if Marcia's dad had taken a turn for the worse, or she'd lost her

job, or she'd been in an accident? None of those things could be Lou's

fault. And if she didn't ring Marcia, might Marcia think that she didn't

care? Lou picked up her mobile and flicked down to the quick dial

number that would bridge the silence between them."

Dee stopped and looked down, feeling her face flush. There

was a hush in the room, but it was a warm kind of hush. Beryl said,

"That's very moving, Dee. I know someone just like Lou."

"It's really easy to picture Lou in the park," said Leon.

"Exposing her vulnerability like that – you do it with such delicacy," said Leila, seeing Dee in an altogether different light.

Even Tessa had to admit, this was the most honest and straightforward writing she'd heard so far on this course.

"It's strong," she said to Dee. "It's a good piece of writing. If you keep this up throughout the story, it'll be publishable. Possibly. Well done."

Dee thought, *they're saying these things about something I've written. Something I've written myself, not copied. Not someone else's stuff that I've taken the credit for. They like my story.*

"Ok everyone, let's wrap it up for tonight, unless anyone's burning to read something?"

The group voted with its feet, getting up and moving to the door in a way that was almost synchronised.

"Nightcap?" Jack asked Beryl, as they brought up the rear. "Got some decent whisky in my room."

"I'd like that," said Beryl.

Jack was staying in a barn conversion annex. His room was quiet and set a little apart from the main building. He led Beryl inside.

"Oh, this is nice," said Beryl. "Did you have to pay for the upgrade?"

"No, I just ticked the *yes* box for disability on the form," said Jack. "They assumed I couldn't walk, or that I used a wheelchair. Got a walk- in shower too. Have a seat."

Beryl settled in a comfortable armchair, while Jack poured two glasses of the single malt. Once they were both seated, Beryl said, "So Jack, if you're not really Jack Harbottle, who are you?"

"I *am* Jack Harbottle," said Jack. "That's the name I was born with. But you may know me as Philip Jensen." He watched her face steadily, clocking her reaction with amusement.

"You're Philip Jensen?" cried Beryl, "the Philip Jensen who writes the Matt Dangerfield series?"

"*That* Philip Jensen," said Jack. "Bet you'd never have guessed that, would you?"

"So what on earth are you doing here?" asked Beryl.

"Research," said Jack. "The next book has Matt undercover spying on a terrorist who's under cover themselves on a writing course. Improbable, I know, but the publishers wanted something a bit different, and I fancied a break."

Beryl burst out laughing. "I'd never have guessed," she said. "But then you've managed to keep a low profile, haven't you? They haven't had you read anything out yet."

"Same could be said of you," said Jack, "so are you going to tell me what *you're* really doing here? And if Beryl's your real name? I hope it is, I've always liked the name Beryl."

"Ok," sighed Beryl. "I'll come clean. But you've to promise not to say anything to anyone. Especially not to Tessa Birnie or Max Logan."

"Promise," said Jack.

Chapter 11

The only light burning after eleven was in Leon's room, as he re-mastered Major Gonzales' mission; but even he had stopped well before midnight. He flossed his teeth and gargled thoroughly with mouthwash. He undressed, washed, and put on the striped pyjamas that his mother had ironed in readiness for his trip. He was curled up in bed and dreaming of rockets blasting into space as Sunday turned into Monday.

Early morning found Tessa warming into her Pilates routine. Afterwards, she assumed the lotus position and meditated, focusing on her inner light. After fifteen minutes, she uncurled herself and slipped on her jogging jacket and trainers. Although she'd never admit it, she found meditation very difficult. Thinking calm and serene thoughts was almost impossible when she knew that Max was in the same building. The house was quiet as she opened the back door and prepared for her daily run. She switched on her iPod shuffle and headed towards the little loch. The early morning air was fresh and slightly misty, the path glistening with dew. It wasn't quite light, but her route was, by now, familiar. Off she jogged, picking up her pace as a running music mix pounded through her headphones. She turned to follow the path of the stream, as she usually did. A dipper darted from one bank to the other, surprised by such an early disturbance. The woodland was gloomy in the half-light, but the path was clear and Tessa jogged on, her mind focusing on her plan for the day. Max could have his way and work on plot. In fact, he could do most of the teaching. She'd do some one to ones, take some extracts to critique, and spend as much time as possible on her novel. It was coming on very well, even if she said so herself. But it was time to ditch Dinah Tannenbaum, she'd decided. Time to find an agent who would value her talent and invest in promoting her.

Had Tessa's mind been on her run and the woodland around her, and had she not had her iPod turned up so high, she might have felt the presence of another, heard the rustle of the undergrowth; but she was oblivious, until it was too late.

It took Beryl several seconds to remember where she was. She turned, and sure enough, there was Jack, still fast asleep. *Well, well,* she thought. *Never thought I'd be in bed with a man again!* And she'd had a good night's sleep and didn't have to get up for a pee once, quite something at her age.

It had seemed like a natural thing to do: they'd shared their stories, sipped at the whisky, and then weariness had overcome them: it had been a strange kind of day.

"Would you like to stay?" Jack had said, "Bed's big enough for two."

Beryl had hesitated for a moment: they were in their seventies and had only just met, and yet here they were, about to spend the night together. Well why not? She wasn't saving herself for anyone, and she liked Jack's company. Close up, and without the distraction of background noise, Jack heard perfectly well, and their conversation had flowed. She liked his way of looking on life – compassionate, gentle, but always seeing the funny side, exposing the folly. He liked that she was self-contained, that she chose her words carefully, that she observed with a dispassionate eye, that the disastrous haircut could, if you weren't careful, distract you from seeing her beautiful, soulful eyes.

"Do you mind if I use your toothbrush?" she'd said, by way of a reply. She hadn't shared a toothbrush since the sixties, and that was in Paris, where manners were somehow different.

"Lucky we've still got our own, eh?" said Jack, pointing the way to the bathroom.

She'd fallen asleep in his arms. His scent took her back to hiding in her father's wardrobe, the same comforting good man smell. It was like coming home.

Leon's dream had been worse than the night before: Major Gonzales had strolled to the launch pad wearing a white dress, just like Marilyn Monroe in *The Seven Year Itch*, and he too was standing over a subway grate, the hair on his legs erect and trembling in the wind from the vent. Leon had woken in a cold sweat. What were his dreams telling him? Should he ring his mother and ask her to arrange for him to see her psychoanalyst? This was terrible: he'd come to Skye to write, to make serious progress with his novel, and here he was, caught up in some unconscious dilemma about his hero's masculinity. If Major Gonzales was an aspect of himself that he was projecting into his writing (the therapy he'd had with his mother's friend Sylvia, who was a Jungian, suggested that all characters were projections of their authors) then what were his dreams saying about him? Somehow he didn't think he could talk to Max or Tessa about it. Maybe he just needed to write his way through it. He stepped into the shower and turned on the cold tap.

Ros was missing Alastair. These courses, these times away from him were something of an ordeal: she yearned for time and a different environment in which to focus on her writing; but she felt as if she'd been cut adrift on some rather murky waters. Alastair always encouraged her to go away, to do these writing programmes. He'd say how good her writing was (although she wasn't altogether sure of how much he had actually read) and he'd enthuse about the benefit she'd derive from these residential weeks. He paid for them with apparent glee: he was so unlike the penny-pinching husbands of her friends, who seemed to resent every little treat they managed to wangle from them. Not her Alastair, though. *You go!* He'd say. *This is what you need to do, this is your work, just like being a barrister's mine. And you need your shots of inspiration more than once a year. Book four, book five courses: we'll soon see you on the Waterstones shelves!* She wasn't entirely sure how he managed when she was away. It wasn't as if he were a very domesticated man. She always left enough dinners in the freezer to keep him going, but she often returned to find that only half had been eaten. He probably ate out, she surmised. Probably went to that little place in the City of which he was so fond. That would be why he usually wasn't in when she phoned him. Of course she liked being able to focus on her writing, but to tell the truth, she did equally well the rest of the year, taking herself off to the British Library. Still, she knew she was lucky to have a husband who encouraged her so well. She'd try to phone him today. If there wasn't a mobile signal, maybe she'd walk into the village to call from the phone box she'd spotted when she and Pamela had gone to the pub, or even see if Megan would let her use the office phone.

Chapter 12

Max woke up feeling groggy. As he opened his eyes and took in the chaos of his room, he remembered the horrors of the day before. Gingerly he tried moving a leg. It worked, so he tried the other. That worked too. He sat up and found that his back was no longer in spasm. He could move with relative ease. This was good. He'd shower and dress, and then talk with Megan and Marcus about changing rooms.

Leila was stuck. She'd set her alarm for five thirty so as to have a good three hours to write before breakfast. Yet her triangle of Fen, Monk, and Tree seemed closed, and she didn't know where to take the narrative. The eternal triangle. The drama triangle. She'd sketched out the plot for the story, but it no longer seemed relevant. Should she introduce another character? Someone to disturb the equilateral nature of her triangle? She decided to paint her toenails.

Pamela wondered how Max was feeling. She showered quickly, sprayed herself liberally with Opium, and dressed in loose green trousers topped with a sunny canary yellow smock. She plugged in her curling tongs and styled her hair, before layering on the make-up that enabled her to face the day and her fellow human beings. Then she headed along the corridor to Max's room and knocked on the door.

Dee was doing sit-ups. She'd let herself go these past few months, and it was time to take herself in hand. She'd already done twenty push-ups, which she felt was quite an achievement. Life seemed brighter this morning. However bizarre yesterday had been, and however difficult she found being amongst a group of strangers – straight strangers at that – she'd begun to feel that maybe she could write, that it wasn't all futile. And her practical common sense had come into its own. After she'd found the mains switch and restored power to the house, people had looked at her differently. Leon had high-fived her when the lights came on, and Megan had given her a little hug. The rest of the group had clapped when the three of them had returned to the dining room. Even Tessa had been approving when she'd read her piece in the evening tutorial, and the comments from the others had seemed genuine enough. She did her last sit-up, and then sat to write her journal. For once there was something upbeat to record. The sun had risen and was shining through her window. This was a perfect little room. She looked forward to telling Nuala all about it.

Maybe they'd even laugh about her deception. It seemed so silly now. Silly and pointless.

Jack woke to find Beryl lying on her side, cupping her face with her hand, smiling at him.

"Morning," he said. "I thought you'd be gone." By the smile on his face, Beryl could tell that he was glad she wasn't.

"I'll go if you like," said Beryl. She reached up to stroke his face. His earlobes were impossibly soft.

"What?" said Jack. "Hold on, let me put my hearing aids in."

"I'll go if you want," repeated Beryl, once the high pitched feedback had died.

"No, I like you being here," he said

"Best night's sleep in years," said Beryl.

"Should do it more often," said Jack.

Marcus was mixing oats, almonds, and dried fruit into a large bowl. He prided himself in offering home-made muesli to his guests.

Besides, it was loads cheaper than the faux-rustic boxes with elegant writing that cost five times as much in the supermarket.

"What are we going to do about Mr Logan's room?" asked Megan.

"I suppose we'll have to clean it up," sighed Marcus.

"We could leave it until they've gone," said Megan.

"He's not going to want to stay in all that mess," said Marcus.

"No, but we could move him," said Megan. "Anna Meredith isn't showing any signs of coming back. He could have her room."

Marcus stroked his chin. Then he nodded. "That's a very good idea," he said. "Why don't you ask Mr Logan if he'd be happy to change?"

"Could you ask him, Marcus?" said Megan. "It's just that…I don't know, something about him makes me feel uncomfortable. I like his books, right enough, but he…"

"Comes onto you? Gives you the creeps?"

"Something like that."

"I'll have a word."

"No, I'd rather you…"

"About the room. I'll ask him about the room."

"Oh. Thanks, Marcus. That'd be great."

"No word from Anna Meredith, then?"

"No. I reckon she'll have caught the ferry to Mallaig, and then gone home."

"Where's she from?"

"Somewhere in England. I'd have to check her form."

"They'd know at the ferry terminal if she'd boarded the boat," said Marcus. "Young Angus, he's got one of those photographic memories. Never forgets a face."

"Are you worried? Do you think she mightn't have gone?"

"There's just been that one sighting in the pub. We don't even know if it was her. We just don't know, Megan, and that's what bothers me. We just don't know."

"But you're happy to move Mr Logan into her room?"

"I suppose so. It's just that…well, I wondered if we should report her missing"

"Try Angus first," said Megan. "Let's leave the polis out of it if we can."

The deer had come out of nowhere, or so it had seemed. It loomed in front of her, as startled by her as she was of it. Tessa stumbled backwards, swerved to avoid the animal, tripped on a tree-root, and rolled down a leafy bank to the edge of the stream. The deer turned and cantered into the woods, noiseless but for the rustle of the leaves under its hooves. Tessa's landing was soft, but she'd ripped something in her ankle. Trying to stand was agony, and there was nothing nearby to hold onto. She shivered. The sweat she'd worked up during her run had cooled and now she felt clammy. Her heart was still racing, partly from the run, partly from shock. How would she ever climb the bank to get back on the path? And what then? She was a good half-mile from the house, and although she could jog that distance in five minutes, she was in no state to walk, let alone run. She reached in her pocket for her iPhone. Damn! She hadn't brought it with her. Besides, there was never a signal out here. Who would miss her? Max wouldn't, that was for sure.

Slowly she sat up. Her right ankle hurt like crazy. She rolled up her trouser leg and saw to her dismay that it was red and swollen. Bruised flesh seemed to be overflowing her trainer like dough rising out of a mixing bowl. She knew not to take her shoe off: chances were she'd never get it back on again. She needed ice, she needed a compression bandage, and she needed to keep the leg elevated: this much she'd learnt from spraining her ankle one school sports day. She also needed to get help. She tried to ease herself on her bottom up the bank, but it was impossible without putting pressure on her foot, and she screamed out loud as the pain shot through her leg. She turned over to see if kneeling was possible. It was painful, but she managed to get onto her hands and knees. If only she could crawl up the bank and onto the path, surely someone would come....

Max heard the knock on his door as he was pulling up his trousers. God, he was dying for a cigarette. First thing he'd do, he'd get that gay guy or the girl to run him down to the village to buy in supplies. Never mind breakfast.

"Who is it?"

"It's me, hun," said Pamela.

Oh God, thought Max. Not her. Anyone but her. And he couldn't bear the term *hun*. If it was short for *honey* it was a ghastly Americanism; but to Max it would always be the slang word for a

German soldier of the First World War, and even Angela Merkel was unlikely to see that as a term of affection.

"I'll see you at breakfast," he said, trying to sound bright.

"I just wanted to see if you were all right," she continued.

"I'm fine!" said Max, putting on his heartiest voice. "Absolutely fine!"

"Are you sure?"

"Oh yes, I'm perfectly fine." As an afterthought he said, "Thank you for asking. Most kind."

Pamela trudged downstairs and contemplated the prunes.

Everyone was quiet, but it was not an oppressive kind of quiet, and Marcus was pleased to see that the group seemed to be gelling. Tessa had yet to appear, but the others were talking in twos or fours, and there was some gentle laughter, he noticed, emanating from the end of the table where Beryl and Jack were sitting.

Pamela cheered when Max entered the room. "Hasn't he done well, everybody?" she exclaimed. Leon and Ros picked up her cheer, although Leila did her best to ignore his presence. Beryl and Jack looked up and smiled. They were not of the whooping generation.

Leon was in earnest conversation with Dee.

"…so I don't know where to take it," he said.

"It's your story," she said. "Major Gonzales is your character. Maybe you need to try him out in different situations?"

"Yeah, could be," he said.

"I'd talk to Max," said Dee, although personally she couldn't stand the man. "He's good at coming up with plots."

"Hate his books, though," said Leon.

"I only read one, and it was ok, but who wants to read about shopping malls in Watford?"

"Pamela, I guess. She loves them."

"Maybe Major Gonzales is asking you to let him express his feminine side more," said Dee, before tucking into her bowl of Marcus's muesli.

"What about Lou? What happens after she rings Marcia?"

"Marcia's not there. She's having sex with Lou's best friend."

"No shit."

"Yeah. Then I had Lou cutting herself. She self harms. But maybe I want her to stop cutting, get a life. You know?"

"So she could just march in and shoot Marcia and her best friend and change her identity and go to another country, start again."

"She wouldn't do that. But the bit about getting a life, yeah, I think that's where I need to take it."

No-one had missed Tessa who was, at this point, attempting to crawl up the bank to the path. Her progress was painfully slow. At last, she reached the top and crawled onto the path. Her hands were filthy, nails broken and grimy with clawing her way up the bank. She was hungry and thirsty. Her ankle throbbed angrily. Tessa crawled to the stump of an ash tree and hauled herself onto it, turning to sit and pause for breath. Surely someone would come looking for her? Max knew that she ran in the mornings, he'd notice that she wasn't there. Or maybe he wouldn't. Maybe he was still incapacitated from his fall. Or maybe he'd see her absence as a lucky break, enabling him to run the programme his way. It was entirely possible that no-one would miss her before evening. Tessa burst into tears.

Chapter 13

"Anyone seen Tessa?" asked Ros, after they'd been sitting in the seminar room for five minutes. "She's not usually late."

"She's probably running, or taking a late shower," said Leila, who had noticed that Tessa had a busy morning routine.

"Where's Max?" asked Leon.

"Gone to the village for fags," said Dee.

"What's that?" asked Jack.

"Max. Gone to village for cigarettes," said Beryl.

"Oh," said Jack. "Where's the other one?"

"We don't know," said Beryl.

Max had persuaded Marcus to drive him into the village, where the general store was open and welcoming, an enticing cornucopia of chocolate and cigarettes. Max hadn't bothered to ask anyone else if they needed anything. He'd been in too much of a hurry to replenish his stash of Marlboros. Marcus needed to stock up on butter, and he'd a few letters for the post. As he chatted to the postmistress, Max stood outside, inhaling deeply. Now all that remained was to confront Tessa about her childish and destructive behaviour. Of course it gave him the upper hand. He chuckled between drags. *Oh yes, Tessa*, he thought, *You've really let yourself down this time.*

On the way to Ardvasar, Marcus had suggested to Max that he move into Anna's room, seeing as the girl was showing no signs of returning.

"It's a nice enough room," said Marcus. "Looks onto the garden, so that's a bonus. A little smaller than the one you've got, that's all."

"Yes, I'll do that," said Max. "Have Megan move my things across."

"Megan's busy today, you'll need to move your own stuff, but we'll clean up the room, you don't need to worry about that."

"If you insist," said Max, thinking that packing up his things and reinstalling him in the other room was the least that they could do. Some people just didn't want to earn their living these days. But moving to a new room was a very welcome offer, and especially one that faced the garden.

They were greeted at the front door by an anxious looking Megan.

"We can't find Ms Birnie," she said. "We've looked everywhere, she's not in her room, nor in the library or the computer room. She didn't come for her breakfast."

"Has anyone seen her at all this morning?" asked Marcus.

"No," said Megan. But the back door was unlocked, so it looks as if she went out for her run.

"Maybe she's fallen into the loch and drowned, and is floating like some pre-Raphaelite corpse as we speak," said Max.

"It's not funny, Mr Logan," said Megan. "I'm worried."

Max was torn between sharing Megan's concern, despite his waspish comment, and being delighted at the thought of Tessa's disappearance. He'd be perfectly happy if he never had to see the woman again, let alone work with her. But he sure as hell wanted to confront her about his room.

"Has anyone traced the path she jogs?" asked Max

"No," said Megan.

"Well, wouldn't that be a good place to start?" asked Max.

"I suppose so," said Megan, feeling as if she'd just been told off.

"I'll go," said Marcus. "Will you come with me, Max?"

"Someone's got to teach the morning seminar," said Max.

"Oh, don't worry about that: Jack's got it in hand," said Megan. "You two were out, and Tessa wasn't around, so Jack offered to run the session."

"That old man with the hearing aids?" said Max, incredulous.

"It seems to be going rather well," said Megan.

"Take a sheet of paper and divide it into three," said Jack.

"It's like being back at school," said Pamela, with a giggle.

"Now write a person's name on one piece, a profession or job role on another, and a place or event on the third. Done it?"

Each person followed Jack's instructions and then nodded when they'd done it.

"Remember consequences?" said Ros

"Passing bits of paper under the desks," said Pamela.

"Fold up each piece of paper, but remember which is which. All the names go in this pile, the jobs over here, and the places at this end. Got it?"

"This is fun," said Dee.

Beryl sat quietly smiling. Jack was doing very well. He tried to play the doddery old man, and there was nothing contrived about his deafness; but he was sharp and bright and funny. Any hint of senility or frailty of mind was part of his little act. The warm-up session had got everyone involved and developing new ideas. Even Leon, with his problematic protagonist, seemed to achieve a breakthrough moment. But Beryl couldn't help wondering what had happened to Tessa. Irritating though the woman was, she seemed to take her responsibility as a tutor seriously and had evidently paid attention to organising the programme for the week. Beryl felt that it was out of character for Tessa simply not to appear. Two disappearances in a week would be too much.

Max and Marcus went out of the back door and took to the path that Max had seen Tessa following. They were strolling where Tessa had jogged, and it took them a good ten minutes to reach the little loch, and a further fifteen to arrive at the stream that meandered through the woodland. They looked around them as they went, but nothing seemed disturbed or strange. They couldn't see footprints on the gravel path: it was impossible to know whether Tessa had followed this route or not.

"What if she went another way?" Max asked.

"She'd have left by the front, I'd have thought," said Marcus, and we're pretty sure that she came this way. Where did you say she was running yesterday?"

"This way," said Max. She was definitely at the loch.

"It makes sense," said Marcus. "If you follow this path through the woods and the azalea grove, you find yourself on the path that leads back to the house. There is another path, but it leads out of the property and up into the hills."

They carried on following the path into the woods.

"Did you hear anything?" Marcus said.

"Just some birds," said Max.

"No, listen," said Marcus. They stopped. This time Max heard it too. Someone was crying. They walked quickly towards the sound, and found Tessa on her tree stump, weeping quietly.

"Well, well, look at you," said Max with a smirk.

"I don't think..." began Marcus.

"I suppose you've come to gloat," said Tessa. "Got your camera, Max?"

"Ms Birnie, I'm glad we've found you," said Marcus, interrupting the spat that seemed inevitable whenever these two were in the same room. "Are you hurt?"

"Of course I'm hurt!" snapped Tessa. "Look!" and she pointed to the ankle which was now huge and purple.

"Oh dearie me," said Marcus. "That does look bad. Can you put any weight on it?"

"No," said Tessa.

"We'll have to carry you," said Marcus.

"I don't think so," said Max. "Not after what I did to my back last night. I'm still recovering. I could send it back into spasm if I'm not careful. Sorry old girl, you're going to have to hop."

"I always could rely on you, Max," sniffed Tessa. "You'll have to get an ambulance down here, Marcus," she added.

"We'll not get a vehicle down here," said Marcus. "I'll have to go back to the house and telephone Dr Macintosh and see if we can get him down with a stretcher or a wheelchair. Come to think of it, I think we've a wheelchair in the house."

"Well how long is that going to take?" cried Tessa, her voice breaking, the bravado that fired her up in the presence of her ex-husband taking flight and leaving her feeling cold, tired, and vulnerable.

"I'll run up to the house just now," said Marcus, "and get back as soon as I can. Mr Logan can stay with you."

"I've got a seminar group to teach," said Max. "You can manage for a few more minutes, can't you Tessa? Besides," he added, looking at Marcus, "after what she did to my room, it wouldn't be safe to leave her alone with me."

"I'd rather spend another hour in this fucking cold wood on my own with a sprained ankle than spend a minute more with you than is necessary," said Tessa. "Just fuck off, Max, go play with the students and pretend you know what you're doing. And what do you mean, after what I did to your room? Leon said something about it last night. Mistook your general chaos for a burglary. Why on earth would I go anywhere near your room?"

"How many years of practice does it take to attain your level of vileness?" asked Max. "And don't play the innocent: you know what I'm talking about."

"You've lost me," said Tessa. "I hope I'm about to lose you."

Max knew Tessa well, knew when she was lying, which she did a lot. She looked genuinely puzzled about his mention of the room, and yet her denials weren't colourful enough to suggest that she was aware of the extent of the vandalism and was dissembling. And had she really been responsible, surely she'd be laughing in his face at the discomfort she must have caused him?

"You mean you don't know about my room?" he said.

"Fuck your room, Max. I don't know who did it over. I'm in pain here, and you're going on about your room: do you think I give a shit?"

"If it wasn't you, who was it?" asked Max.

"Oh, do shut the fuck up, Max, and get me some help."

Chapter 14

Max and Marcus sprinted back to the house. To be more exact, Marcus sprinted, Max walked as briskly as he could behind. The morning session had ended, and Megan had thought on her feet and provided coffee and cake for everyone. There was a loud and lively buzz: the group had enjoyed Jack's session, and had found the exercise with the three piles of paper to be fun and illuminating.

"So if Major Gonzales found himself in a chip shop with a mission to recycle half the rubbish in Wensleydale, I'd have a whole new strand to my story," Leon was saying to Leila.

No-one had really missed Tessa, but they were reminded, by the breathless entrance of Max and Marcus, of her strange disappearance.

"Did you find Tessa?" asked Beryl, her coffee cup poised above its saucer.

"Aye, we did," said Marcus. "She's twisted her ankle badly. Fell during her run. We'll be calling for the doctor, and we need some help to move her from the woods to here."

"Happy to be of service," said Major Gonzales, via Leon, having now edged closer to the integration of the Major's male, testosterone-driven aspect and his emotionally intelligent, caring feminine side.

"I don't mind giving a hand," said Leila, though what exactly she could do, she wasn't sure: she thought it incumbent upon her to offer some assistance, and she thought that Dinah would expect no less from her protégée.

"We need to get a wheelchair down to the woods," said Marcus. "I think there's one in the outhouse. And we need to call Dr Mackintosh."

"There's one in the back of the annexe," said Jack. "I noticed it when I was unpacking. Strange thing to come upon. If you're disabled, on the whole, you know it before setting out for here, and chances are, you'll bring your own wheelchair. But there's one there, and it sounds like Tessa could do with it."

Leila, Marcus, and Major Gonzales headed back down the path to the lake, alongside the stream, and into the woods. They took it in turns to push the wheelchair, an old fashioned NHS model with four small wheels and no means for the occupant to propel themselves.

"What kind of state's she in?" asked Leila, slightly fearful of messy physical injury.

"She's upset, naturally, and tired, and she'll be cold by now," said Marcus. "And her ankle looks sore and swollen – the doctor will want to take a good look."

"Should we have brought blankets and painkillers?" asked Leon.

"I've a blanket," said Marcus. "We'll leave it to the doctor to prescribe medication."

They arrived at the tree stump where Marcus and Max had left Tessa. Marcus was quite sure it was the right place. But there was no sign of Tessa. He called, in case she'd crawled off to have a pee in the undergrowth.

"Tessa!" he called. "We're here with your chair." There was no response. Just the twittering of a few birds and the rustle of the dying leaves in the breeze.

"We left her here!" Marcus exclaimed, as Leila and Leon glared at him in disbelief. "She can't have gone far: that ankle was angry and swollen and getting worse. She must be here somewhere."

"This is all part of some kind of plot, isn't it?" said Leila. "You're putting us in challenging situations to see what we make of them and how we integrate them into our fiction, isn't that so?"

"No, it isn't so," said Marcus, trying hard to keep his own panic at bay. Where the hell had Tessa Birnie gone? How had she gone? The woman was in agony, she couldn't possibly have moved without assistance.

"Is there a history of sightings of UFOs in this part of the island?" asked Leon.

"Oh, for God's sake, get real," said Marcus. "What have UFO sightings got to do with a missing woman – two missing women?"

"There's more documentation than the government would ever admit about alien abductions," said Leon. "It happens all the time, only the authorities keep a lid on it and try to stop us from finding out who and what are really out there," added Leon.

"That's such crap," said Leila. "Hadn't we better spread out and look for Tessa? If she's delirious and wandered off, she could be anywhere."

"The aurora borealis is good enough for us," said Marcus; "but there are no flying saucers. Leila's right: we need to spread out and try to find out where she's gone."

Jack was telling Max about the morning session. "It worked well enough, getting them to work on their imaginations, leaving their works in progress behind," said Jack. "They're having free time now until after the coffee break."

"Nice one," said Max. "I'll take over from here. We'll work the rest of the morning on plot, and then start this afternoon by looking at some of the archetypal stories that form the backbone of fiction."

"Well that sounds ambitious," said Jack. "I'll look forward to it." He thought he might suggest a siesta to Beryl.

Dee was typing enthusiastically into her laptop. When Ros came over for a chat, Dee said, "sorry Ros, but I'm changing the focus of the story. Last night, and then my talk with Leon, has given me a whole new take on Lou and her story. So you won't mind if I'm not up for a chat."

Ros gave a peeved little sniff and turned away. With Leon and Leila out on their rescue mission, there wasn't really anyone to talk with. Just the unbearable Pamela, and Beryl, who seemed not to have very much to say. Still, it was Beryl she approached when she was looking for somewhere to sit and drink her morning coffee.

"It isn't quite as I expected," she said.

"Oh? And how is that?" replied Beryl.

"I'd expected something more organised, an environment geared for us to focus on our creativity," said Ros.

"And this course isn't enabling you to do that?" said Beryl.

"No, it really isn't," said Ros.

"That's a shame," said Beryl. "What is it that's not working for you?"

"Well, there's the spatting between Tessa and Max for a start," said Ros, "and then there's the disappearance of Anna – which has never, if you ask me, been pursued with the vigour I'd expect from a place like this – and then there's the business with the lights, and now this, with Tessa."

"It sounds like Tessa's fallen on some tree roots," said Beryl. "I'm sure there's nothing untoward lurking in the woods."

What Beryl didn't say was that she was, by now, pretty sure that something rather unpleasant and definitely sinister was working its sorcery upon the house.

Chapter 15

Ros decided it was time to phone Alastair. She walked into the office where Megan was filing some forms.

"Would it be possible to use the office phone?" asked Ros. "There doesn't seem to be a mobile signal anywhere in the house or grounds, and I do need to check that everything's all right at home. Or I can walk down to the village."

Megan hesitated. One of the house rules was that the office phone was for official use only; but the nearest public telephone was by the post office, and she was aware that this course was not going as smoothly as it should. There would be some merit in allowing students to use the office phone where she could overhear what they were reporting home. She also reasoned that people were less likely to be overtly critical if they knew that one of the Creative Hub staff was within earshot.

"Of course you can," she said to Ros, and then felt humbled at the sight of Ros's face lighting up like a child's at Christmas.

"Really? Oh Megan, that's so kind of you. Thank you." Ros scooted round to the desk and Megan moved aside to make room for her.

"I'll just go and put the tatties on for lunch," she said.

Ros dialled Alastair's office number. She didn't think he was due to be in court this week, so that was where she'd be most likely to find him. It rang three times before going to voicemail. Ros was surprised: normally Lana, his secretary, would pick up after one ring. Maybe they were both in a meeting. She left a message, and then thought she'd try their home number: he did occasionally prepare his briefs at home when he needed not to be disturbed.

Megan returned as Ros was waiting for the phone to be answered. Finally someone picked up. Only it wasn't Alastair, and neither was it Bella, the Ukranian girl they employed (unofficially, of course, and at below minimum wage) to clean their comfortable house in Walton upon Thames. Megan saw Ros's face widen into disbelief, and then crumple, as, after a few words, Ros slammed down the phone and ran sobbing from the room.

Tessa couldn't have made it up. Moments after Max and Marcus had strolled away, rescue arrived on two wheels and a rather handsome pair of legs. Mounting was a little tricky, but once she was seated, despite the fact that the pain in her ankle continued to burn and throb, she knew that events were taking a turn for the better.

"His secretary!" cried Ros. "Of all the clichéd, stupid, pathetic things! And there was I, cooking his little dinners, making sure he had a week's worth of clean underpants, and all the time he was just waiting for the coast to be clear so that he could turn our home – our home! – into his sordid little love-nest."

"It's awful, just awful," said Pamela, not knowing what else to say.

"They must have been at it for well over a year," said Ros. "He started packing me off on my writing courses about eighteen months ago. Come to think of it, that was about the time that Lana joined his office. Crafty little bitch. What does he see in her?"

"He's probably having his male menopause," said Pamela.

"Well he can go and have it somewhere else," said Ros.

"Are you sure?" asked Pamela, "Did he sound very sorry?"

"I didn't wait for him to speak to me," said Ros. "Hearing that woman answer the phone in my house was enough."

"Are you sure they weren't working?" asked Pamela, who always hoped for happy endings.

"No, no, they weren't working. Oh, I should have realised. It's not as if it's the first time. Stupid! I'm so stupid!"

"Oh, don't say that, hun," said Pamela. "It's not your fault."

"But what if it is? What if he just doesn't find me attractive any more? What if no-one will find me attractive ever again?" and Ros burst into tears again.

Megan, realising that Ros's phone call had not gone well, made her and Pamela a cup of tea. After all, it was what you did when people were upset. She wondered what people did in countries where tea drinking was not the cultural norm that it was in Britain. She put a little pile of digestive biscuits onto a plate, and carried it all into the living room where Pamela was consoling Ros.

"Anything I can do?" she said, as she placed the tea and biscuits on the coffee table.

"Nothing short of homicide," said Ros, and then blew her nose loudly. "Except that I'm going to kill him myself."

Dee walked into the room, having heard the raised voices. She was giving herself a break to stretch and find some coffee.

"Hey Ros, what's up?" she asked.

"Nothing," said Ros, deciding that the fewer people who knew of her humiliation, the better. "Just some bad news from home."

"Her old man's having it off with his secretary," said Pamela.

Ros glared at the stupid woman and regretted having taken her into her confidence. Had she no discretion? Now everyone would know, and they'd all pretend to feel sorry for her, but they'd be laughing behind her back.

"Thank you, Pamela," she said. "I'd rather you didn't talk about my business to the others."

"Sorry hun," said Pamela. "I was only trying to help."

"Spreading gossip doesn't help," said Ros, and left the room with as much dignity as she could muster. As she reached the door, she turned back to Pamela.

"And for fuck's sake, stop calling me hun!"

Leila, Marcus, and Leon burst through the back door bringing with them a chill blast of earthy woodland air. Megan looked up from the vegetables she was chopping.

"Where is she?" she asked.

"She's gone!" said Marcus.

"Gone?"

"We got there, and she'd vanished."

"But I thought she'd hurt her ankle?"

"She had! There's no way she could have walked on it."

"So where's she gone?"

"If we knew that, we wouldn't be panicking!" said Marcus. "I think we need to call the group together."

"Why not talk to Mr Logan first?" suggested Megan.

"What would be the point?" snapped Leila. "They hate each other."

"But he knows her better than anyone. They used to be married."

"Ok," said Marcus. "Fetch him in."

Max was enjoying a cigarette in the rose garden. It was peaceful without Tessa being constantly on his back, and the old man had done a good job this morning. If they had to bus Tessa back to London, he wouldn't mind finishing off the course with Jack. He could probably get him to take on the lion's share of the work. Seemed to welcome feeling useful. Funny, though: Max was sure he'd seen him somewhere before. He looked familiar, but when Max had asked him, the old man had said no, he didn't think they'd met before.

"Mr Logan, we need you in the house," said Marcus.

"Is she back?" asked Max, taking a last drag from his cigarette.

"No, that's the thing," said Marcus. "We can't find her."

Max choked on his smoke and then laughed. "Well, how'd you manage that?" he said. "She sticks like Velcro, that one."

"I don't think it's a laughing matter," said Marcus. "She's injured, but we cannae find her anywhere."

"Abducted by aliens?" said Max. "Don't panic, an hour in her poisonous company and they'll be beaming her back down to earth and fleeing to the farthest galaxy to get away from her." He chuckled to himself at the thought of Tessa in the hands of aliens.

"That's what I've been saying," said Leon, who had joined the pair. "We just don't know what's out there. She could be on her way to a far galaxy as we speak!

"Oh, grow up!" said Max. "No, it was probably all put on in the first place. She was playing the sympathy card, and when we didn't get back quickly enough for her, she got bored and legged it."

Marcus gave up on Max and swept back into the house. He'd had enough. This was the absolute limit. He'd hand in his resignation and go back to Edinburgh, face the music, do what he needed to do. Anything to get him away from this lonely place with its midges and mischief. In the kitchen, he opened one of the top cupboards and pulled out a bottle of Talisker. He kept it for emergencies and special occasions. If this wasn't an emergency, he didn't know what was. Megan turned from her vegetables.

"Make that two," she said. "Marcus, what are we to do?"

Chapter 16

Malcolm the postie liked to take a short cut across the Creative
Hub's land. He knew he shouldn't, but the folk who worked there were
nice enough and didn't seem to mind. It reduced the time his round
took, and put him in a mellow mood, because woodland was like that.
It always made you feel better to be amongst trees. It was a shame that
more people didn't know that, Malcolm thought. The world might be a
more peaceful place if people just went and hung out in forests more
often. He liked the little stream and the dippers that flitted from rock to
rock. If he was lucky, he'd catch sight of a goldfinch or two. He didn't
often meet anyone as he cycled the path through the woods.
Occasionally, one of the centre's visitors was down by the loch, but he
generally had the place to himself.

He almost fell off his bike when he saw the woman sitting on
the tree stump. She was crying and looked like she'd been attacked.
He stopped, dismounted, and went over to her, though he was careful
not to get too close, in case someone had…well, in case the last thing
she needed to see right now was a man.

"Hello," he said.

"Hello," said Tessa.

"What happened to you?"

"I tripped and fell," said Tessa. "Stupid, isn't it? They said they'd come back with a chair, but they've been gone ages."

"That ankle doesn't look good," said Malcolm, who'd done a bit of volunteering for the St John's Ambulance when he was at school.

"It hurts," said Tessa. "It hurts a lot. And I'm so cold." She started to cry again.

"We'd better get you away from here, then," said Malcolm as he took off his jacket. "May I put this around you?"

"Yes please," said Tessa. He was very kind, this young postman, but she didn't see how he planned to get her away.

"Now, I'd like you to put your arm around my shoulder," said Malcolm, "so that you're standing on your good leg. That's it." Tessa allowed him to pull her into standing, so that she was leaning into the sturdy stranger. "Ok," said Malcolm, "now we'll hop over to my bike, and you're to sit on it."

"Are you sure?" said Tessa.

"It's the only way," said Malcolm. "Then I'll wheel you straight to the doctor's. It'll take us half an hour, will that be ok?"

"Oh yes," said Tessa. Anything was better than sitting here waiting for that useless Marcus to take her back to the house for Max to gloat at her. Besides, she didn't see how she'd get upstairs to her room. "Do you have letters to deliver?" she asked, as an afterthought.

"Only to the Creative Hub now," said Malcolm, "and I can do that once I've made sure that you're being looked after."

"You're being very kind," said Tessa. "Thank you." It wasn't often that she had reason to express gratitude to anyone, but this young man was saving her life. "I'm Tessa. Tessa Birnie. Maybe you've read my books?"

"Glad to meet you, Tessa Birnie," he said. "I'm Malcolm. What kind of books?"

"Literary fiction," said Tessa.

"I'm more of a sci-fi man myself," said Malcolm. "Still, you never know, maybe they'll have one of yours in the library. I'll give it a go."

She watched Max moving from one room to another. Of course she maintained a discrete distance and could only see shadows through the window. But it was clear enough what was happening: it was all going to plan. She smiled, and popped a chocolate button into her mouth.

"I really don't have a choice, Megan," said Marcus. "I have to call the polis."

"We don't want them crawling all over the place, though," said Megan.

"Why, d'you have something to hide?"

"Not really…"

"Look, they won't be interested in your little stash. Just stick it in the herb cupboard, they'll never know the difference."

"It's not that…"

"Well what? They're more likely to be interested in me than you, that's if they make the connection."

"And they might."

"Aye, they might; but there aren't any bodies, unless there's something you're not telling me. It'll just be a missing persons thing. Sorry Megan, but I think we have to take the risk."

Megan gnawed at a cuticle. It was all going wrong. That wretched woman and her lecherous ex-husband were spoiling it all. Well, Megan had no intention of letting them succeed. No, they'd soon find out Megan Kennedy was made of, and they wouldn't like it. They wouldn't like it one tiny bit.

Ros was thinking about how she'd do it. She wasn't good with blood, so stabbing was out. She wouldn't know where to get a gun, still less what to do with one. Poison was an option, she could cook him a nice beef casserole, laced with lethal mushrooms; she was sure that the woods hereabouts were full of fungi that would finish a person off; but the result could be messy. Suffocation with a pillow appealed, in that it would lead to a fairly quick death without blood or vomit. She could do it while he was asleep. But Alastair worked out and he'd be strong enough to push her off if he awoke. She could fake a burglary, bash him over the head with one of his golf clubs, then set up the scene, smash a window, call the police, play the grieving widow; but then there was the problem of blood again. And besides, the police usually saw through faked burglaries. Something about the way the glass fell. She could cut the brake cables on his BMW, only she didn't know what a brake cable looked like, and she didn't know where you'd find them. Cars these days seemed full of wires and electronic gadgets, or so she'd gleaned from that awful motoring programme he insisted on watching on television. She could wait until he was in his bath and drop in an electric heater, or better still, her hairdryer; but suspicion would fall upon her immediately. She could make it look like suicide and fake a note – she was good at forging his signature; but the problem remained: how to do it? Wrist slashing was out – blood again – and overdoses were messy: she didn't want to risk vomit on her nice new carpet. They'd only had it fitted last month.

"Penny for them," said Pamela, finding Ros lost in thought.

"Just wondering what to do about Alastair," said Ros, annoyed at the interruption.

"There's always marriage guidance," said Pamela.

"I think we're past that," said Ros, wondering how those poison tipped umbrellas worked.

"Then you need a good lawyer," said Pamela. "Get out, get as much as you can screw out of him, start again."

"Hmm," said Ros, mostly to shut Pamela up. Death had to be the answer. She had to come up with an effective and efficient way of dispatching him.

"How about bunking off this afternoon?" Jack said to Beryl.

"What did you have in mind?" asked Beryl.

"A siesta," said Jack.

Beryl couldn't remember when she'd last been propositioned at all, let alone with such seductive charm. Unfortunately, she had her job to do.

"Not today," she said. "I'm interested to see how the afternoon pans out, and what Max does with the archetypes."

"Spoilsport," said Jack. "You should take your chance, you know. Who knows if we'll still be here tomorrow, what with our age and all the disappearances."

"I love it when you're cheerful," said Beryl.

He wheeled her back along the path the way he'd come. Where Tessa would have turned right and back into the Creative Hub's gardens, Malcolm turned left, crossed the stream by a little bridge, and then steered his bike and Tessa onto a narrow lane that led into the back of the village. He was very careful not to knock her injured leg.

They arrived at the doctor's house, which doubled as his surgery, after half an hour. Tessa dismounted slowly, holding on to Malcolm for balance. He helped her to hop into the house.

"Good morning, Hazel," he said to the woman sitting at the reception desk.

"Now what have you got there, Malcolm?" Hazel McLure sat behind the desk, reading glasses dangling from a gold chain below her breasts, tight grey curls cut sensibly short. She'd known Malcolm since he was born.

"This is Tessa Birnie," he said. "She was running in the woods and tripped and fell. I think her ankle's sprained. She's from up at the Hub."

"Oh, I see," said Hazel, as if Tessa's being resident at the Creative Hub had something to do with her misadventure. "Well Malcolm, you've brought her to the right place. Now tell me, how's your mother?"

"She's fine, right enough," said Malcolm, easing Tessa into a chair, and placing another one in front of her. "Can I lift your leg onto the chair?" he asked. "It's best to elevate it."

This man is an angel, thought Tessa, and then winced as he lifted the injured leg, by now inflamed and stiff, onto the chair.

"Do you have any ice, Hazel?" he asked the receptionist.

"You'll get some at the Hotel," she said.

"Right-o," he said. "I'll away to get some."

"What a nice man," Tessa said to Hazel, after he'd left.

"Aye, he's one of the best," said Hazel. "Known him since he was a wee boy, and he's always been the same."

Moments later, Malcolm was back with a bag full of ice. He placed it on Tessa's ankle. "That'll help the swelling," he said. "I'll wait with you 'til you've seen the doctor."

"Don't you need to finish your round?" asked Tessa.

"No, it'll wait," he said.

Dr Mackintosh sighed. Another casualty from that house full of weirdos. If he got paid for ministering to them, he'd be a rich man by now; but no, it was all on the National Health, he wouldn't get a penny extra.

"Let's have a look now," he said, rolling up Tessa's trouser leg and untying her trainer. She cried out as he took her shoe off.

Dr Mackintosh felt around the swelling and got Tessa to wiggle her toes.

"Good," he said, "nothing broken. We'll just strap it up for you. Have you used crutches before?"

"I'll take you back," said Malcolm.

"I don't know if I can manage the bike again," said Tessa.

"I'll fetch my car, I'll just be five minutes."

"I don't know how to thank you," said Tessa.

"We'll think of something," said Malcolm.

Marcus dialled the number for the local police station.

"So you'll come to the house?" he was saying, as Megan came into the office. "Aye, we'll see you this afternoon. Yes, I know you're out at Portree. Aye, we'll call if she turns up."

"Will we tell them about Anna Meredith?" asked Megan.

"I guess we should," said Marcus. "D'you think the two disappearances are connected?"

"I just don't know," said Megan.

Max had moved his belongings into the room that Anna Meredith had occupied for such a short time. The room was smaller than his other one, but it was sunnier and looked onto the garden. If Tessa failed to materialise, he'd move into her room with the big bed. He couldn't be doing with single beds, he'd have to have words with the programme organisers about the lack of appropriate facilities.

There was a fine layer of dust on the dressing table, shown up by the midday sunshine. He found himself thinking about Anna Meredith. He had met her before, he remembered it all too clearly now. That summer at Vibrant Waters had been his last there before the regime change. Anna had seemed to soak in every word he'd said in the tutorials, wherever he looked, there she was. The other girls were either spoken for or even plainer than Anna. He thought he'd been doing her a favour.

Beryl sat with Jack on a bench on the lawn. The day had turned warm, unseasonably so, and they were both enjoying the sun on their faces.

"You'll not be short of material," said Beryl.

"Oh no, the book's coming along very nicely," said Jack. "But you still haven't told me what you're doing here. Something tells me you're not here to learn about novel writing techniques."

"There's always something interesting to glean on these courses," said Beryl.

"Well, if you don't come clean, you're sleeping on your own tonight," said Jack.

"You're a hard man," said Beryl, laughing. "All right, I'll tell you. But you're not to breathe a word. Promise?"

"I think I already did, but we got interrupted," said Jack.

Beryl looked around to check that no-one was within listening distance.

"Well, you see," she started, but was cut short by the sight of Leon running out.

"They've called the police," he called. "Tessa's disappeared."

"We'd better go and see what's happening," said Beryl. "Let's finish this conversation later."

They rose and turned towards the house.

Chapter 17

Malcolm helped Tessa into his Fiesta. He put the crutches in the back seat.

"You won't mind if we stop off at my place?" he said, once she was belted in. "There's just a wee job I need to do."

"Ok," said Tessa. She didn't care if the others were worrying about her. In fact, she hoped they were. It would serve Max right, and the students might appreciate her a little more if they had to suffer an extra session or two with him. They'd realise how lucky they were that she was the lead tutor on the course.

Malcolm drove out of the village in the opposite direction to the Creative Hub. He pulled up in front of a small, squat cottage that sat on its own in a garden that looked only partially tended. A bed of lettuces had bolted, and there were dandelions in the straggly lawn. He got out of the car and went to open the passenger door. He took the crutches from the back and held them for Tessa.

"Shall I just wait in the car for you?" she said, tired now.

"There's something I'd like to show you," said Malcolm. "And wouldn't you like a nice cup of tea?"

Tessa was torn between wanting to get back to her room so that she could lie down and rest, and the tempting offer of tea. Besides, she didn't want to offend this kind young man, her personal Good Samaritan.

"Ok," she said. "Just a quick one." She followed him up the path to the front door. Its green paint was flaky and he seemed to have trouble with the key. She was awkward with the crutches, and hobbled slowly behind him. He held the door open. It creaked on its hinges.

"Welcome," he said, and ushered her into a dark and dusty interior.

"Phone call for you," Megan said to Ros. "It's a man."

"It'll be Alastair. I don't want to talk to him," said Ros.

"Well, you'll have to tell him," said Megan, holding out the phone to her.

Ros sighed heavily and marched up to the desk, snatching the phone from Megan.

"I've got nothing to say to you," Megan heard her say, before discretely leaving the office. Yet it was several minutes before Ros herself emerged. Megan had busied herself in the kitchen, tidying up after lunch. She looked up as Ros came in to fetch a glass of water. Her hand shook as she turned the tap.

"Everything ok?" asked Megan.

"No, everything is not ok," said Ros, who felt like slapping the silly young woman who clearly didn't have a clue about the havoc wreaked by an unfaithful spouse, especially when you, the one who had been betrayed, were in your early fifties and feeling as if you were long past your sell-by date. In fact, she felt that she was surrounded by people who simply didn't understand. She had never felt lonelier. She needed to talk with someone about what to do next, about how to deal with her husband's insistence that she'd misunderstood the situation, that there was a perfectly innocent explanation as to why Lana had been at the house, and how he was on his way to Skye to talk with her in person.

"I don't want you to come," she'd said to him, dreading such a public confrontation. "It's over, as far as I'm concerned, Alastair, and I shall be seeking legal advice as soon as I return to Walton on Thames."

As usual, he hadn't listened to her, and had continued to insist that his bag was packed and he would be with her by lunch-time tomorrow.

She went to sit in the library where she hoped to be left alone to compose herself; but no sooner had she settled into a leather armchair than Pamela swept in.

"There you are, hun," said Pamela. "I heard that you'd had a phone call. Not bad news I hope?"

"Just Alastair," said Ros.

"Called to apologise?" asked Pamela.

"Called to deny that there was anything to apologise about," said Ros.

"Well, that's good news, then," said Pamela.

Ros didn't reply. Some people were beyond stupid.

"It *is* good news, isn't it?" asked Pamela.

"No, it isn't," said Ros. "He's on his way here, and I don't want to see him and I most certainly don't want to listen to any more of his lies."

"What if he's telling the truth?" asked Pamela.

"Are you really that stupid?" said Ros. "Of course he's not telling the truth. He's having an affair with his secretary. He's trying to limit the damage that a divorce will lead to. He knows he'll lose the house and half of his money, so he's trying to persuade me that nothing's going on, it's all about me having a vivid imagination, and Lana was helping him with a complicated case."

"I don't think you need to be rude to me, Ros," said Pamela. "It's not called for. I'm only trying to help."

"What on earth do you think you can do to help?" Ros was shouting now. "Have you been in my situation? Did you ever have a husband cheat on you repeatedly until he overstepped the mark and you reached the point where you couldn't – wouldn't – take any more? No, I shouldn't think your relationships have ever extended beyond one night stands."

Megan had heard the shouting and come to the door. She watched as Pamela turned white, tears forming in her eyes and then streaming down her face.

"At least your husband's still alive," said Pamela, and hurried from the room.

Max was getting ready for the afternoon session. He hadn't felt very hungry, so had a nicotine lunch in the rose garden. He hardly wanted to admit it to himself, but he was worried about Tessa. The woman was abominable, and he loathed almost everything about her (although she'd been quite the little tigress in her youth before she stopped smoking); but he didn't wish her any harm, or at least no more than the odd public humiliation or book flop. There was still no sign of her, and the police were taking their time in getting to the house. Still, he'd better keep things going and teach this lacklustre group of students something. Of course the anticipation of an afternoon in Leila's company was very pleasant, and he looked forward to hearing her read some more from her novel, dreary though it was. He also had an exercise for them involving kitchen implements and newspapers. He'd got Marcus to lend him a couple of different sized knives, a bottle of wine, and some newspaper. He intended to get the group thinking about plot in crime scenes. He laid the newspapers on the chair and the knives alongside each other on the large table around which everyone would be sitting. He set the bottle of wine – a rather nice burgundy, he noticed - on the table, and went out for a last smoke before calling everyone together.

When he got back to the rose garden, he was annoyed to find Pamela on his favourite bench; but as he approached her, he saw that she had been crying. She'd looked up and seen him, so he felt he had to say something.

"Anything wrong, Pamela?"

"Hello Max. No, nothing really. Just something Ros said."

"Sorry to hear that."

"I don't suppose you could give me a cigarette?" she said.

"Didn't know you smoked," said Max, handing her the packet.

"I don't," she said. "Not any more. Not often, anyway. Thanks."

He lit the cigarette for her and wondered what that snooty woman from Walton on Thames could have said to have deflated Pamela so. For once she made no effort to flirt with him. God! These women! A chap never knew where he stood with them. They were, on the whole, nothing but trouble, and totally incomprehensible.

"Time to get started," he said, after they'd finished smoking.

Max was first into the seminar room, and the sight that met him filled him with horror. Someone had spread the newspapers across the table. In the middle, was a photograph of Max himself, a rather handsome publicity shot of which he was quite fond; but whoever had set up this scene had slashed across it and left the knife – the larger of the two he'd borrowed from Marcus – stabbed through the centre. All around was red, giving the appearance of blood having leaked from the photograph; but Max realised that it was the red wine that he'd brought in: someone had poured it across the table and left the bottle on its side, empty, as the liquid soaked into the newspaper, spread, and dripped onto the floor, spoiling the old carpet with a bloody stain.

The students started to arrive. Leon was the first.

"Hey, Max, that's brilliant!" he said. "Do we have to guess who dunnit?"

"God that's horrible," said Leila. "Look what a mess you've made of the carpet, Max. Don't you think it's a bit much?"

"Quite a tableau, Max," said Beryl, thinking that maybe the man did have some enthusiasm for his task after all.

"Bloody waste of good wine," said Jack, peering at the label on the overturned bottle. "Hope you decanted it and this is just cochineal."

Dee didn't know what to make of the scene, and in fact found it rather disturbing.

Pamela gasped as she looked at the table. "When did you do that, Max?" she asked. "It's certainly gruesome. Is it from your next book?"

Ros didn't come to the session – she'd gone to lie down and think about the possibilities that driving back to Walton on Thames with Alastair might give her. A misadventure at a motorway service station, or a staged carjacking in a minor road opened up a whole new range of choices.

"Which one of you has done this?" Max asked, his voice devoid of its usual bluster.

No-one answered.

"Come on," said Max. "It's very clever, and you've got the session off to a lively start, but it's time to come clean."

"You set it up, didn't you?" said Pamela. "Didn't you do it before going for your cigarette?"

"No," said Max. The room was silent. "Someone's idea of a joke?" asked Max. He was beginning to feel nervous. First his room, now this. And it couldn't be Tessa. At least, he didn't think it could.

Beryl watched the group. Each face looked troubled. None looked guilty, or satisfied, or mischievous. She feared that things were getting seriously out of hand.

Chapter 18

Marcus took a deep breath and headed for the front door. Two police constables stood on the step. The man was a redhead, well-built and ruddy with large, freckled hands. The woman was shorter, slimmer, brown hair clipped neatly back.

"We've come about the missing person," said Andy MacLeod.

"Aye, Tessa Birnie, one of the tutors," said Marcus. "Come on in."

The constables followed Marcus into the office. He indicated the two visitor chairs and then moved a safe distance away to take his place behind the desk.

"She went for a run down to the woods, fell and hurt her ankle. We found her sitting there around 10.00am. We came back to the house to fetch a wheelchair, and when we got back she'd vanished."

Lindsay Lennox took down notes in her pad.

"Who's *we*, if you don't mind my asking?" asked Constable MacLeod. "You said *we* found her."

"I did," said Marcus. "And Max Logan, who's also teaching on the programme."

"So what happened when you went back?"

"I went back with two of the students. Leon Waterson and Leila Morris."

"Max Logan didn't go with you?"

"He'd hurt his back and didn't want to risk putting it out by lifting Ms Birnie or pushing the chair."

"And how was she when you found her?"

"In pain. I'd guess she'd sprained her ankle. She couldn't stand on it and she couldn't walk."

"But when you went back she'd gone?"

"Vanished. No trace of her. We looked everywhere."

"Have you searched the house?"

"We've looked in all the obvious places; but she couldn't have got back here without our noticing."

"We'll need to look at her room."

"Of course."

"And talk to the staff and visitors."

"That shouldn't be a problem."

"Does she know anyone on the island?" asked Lindsay.

"I don't know," said Marcus. "I don't think so."

"Right, let's take a look," said Andy, and the two constables stood up to begin their search.

Marcus led them upstairs to the garden room. He opened the door with his master key. Tessa's room was tidy. Her laptop sat closed upon the desk, and her pilates mat was rolled up and neatly placed in the corner. Her iPhone was on the bedside table next to the bottle of Jo Malone body lotion. Lindsay Lennox picked up the phone and looked at the screen.

"Useless for signals, this place," she said, noting that there was no signal and no waiting messages.

"Everything looks in order," said Andy. It seemed clear to him that Tessa had expected to return. He peered into the en-suite bathroom. The woman was neat, that was for sure. Towels folded neatly, basin clean, toilet lid down. "We'll go and talk to the others," he said. "Let's talk to Max Logan first, as he was one of the last to see her. Then we'll have a chat with those two students who went out with you."

Marcus went to look for Max.

Beryl had helped Max to sit down while Pamela went to fetch him some water.

"If this is someone's idea of a prank, it's gone beyond funny," said Max.

Leon thought that Major Gonzales would have an ingenious plan to catch the trickster, and he wished he could think what it would be. He thought that maybe Gonzales would keep everyone in the room and refuse to let them out, refuse them access to food or drink until the culprit confessed. Leon's money was on Pamela: she was so unlikely that she just might have done it, possibly as research for her Croydon murder story. And she had looked upset earlier on. If not Pamela, then Leila. She hated Max. But was she bothered enough to go to these extreme and dramatic lengths?

Jack rather fancied mousy Megan for the prank: there was something about that girl. She looked the innocent with her discrete little nose piercing and her tie-dyed headband; but he sensed that she wasn't quite what she seemed.

Everyone was occupied: Marcus with the police, Max and the group with the splendid scene she'd set up in the seminar room. No-one noticed her flitting past the French windows. She'd found a way of exploiting being invisible to her advantage: it was almost like being a magician. Things were working out very nicely, she thought, as she popped a chocolate button into her mouth. She waited until Megan had gone into the garden to cut some herbs, and then she slipped into the house.

Andy MacLeod and Lindsay Lennox found Max surrounded by students in the seminar room. Three appeared to be ministering to him, with the others sitting around a table on which was displayed a grim tableau.

"Mr Logan?" said Andy, "Mind if we have a word?"

Max sighed, brushed his floppy fringe out of his eyes, stood up, and followed the constables into the library.

"We're looking into Ms Birnie's disappearance," said Lindsay. "It seems that you were one of the last to have seen her. What did you notice?"

"She'd hurt her ankle, she was making a fuss, we said we'd come back to call the doctor, but decided to take a wheelchair down there ourselves. Or rather, Marcus Dean was to take the chair down with a couple of the students."

"And what did you do after getting back to the house?" asked Andy.

"I changed rooms," said Max. "Someone vandalised my room, so I moved into one that had become vacant."

"Who do you think vandalised your room, sir?" asked Lindsay.

"I assumed it was Tessa, but she denied it," said Max.

"Why would Ms Birnie want to vandalise your room?" asked Andy.

"We were married," said Max, and immediately wished he'd said nothing: both constables' heads jerked up, and he knew that they were thinking that this may turn out to be more than a missing persons enquiry.

"A long time ago," continued Max. "Water under the bridge. Both moved on."

"But you thought she might have vandalised your room?"

"I couldn't think who else would," said Max. "It's not what you expect when you come to teach on these programmes."

"Would you mind if we had a look at the room you left?" asked Andy.

"Be my guest," said Max. "But I'm not so sure now that it was Tessa. I confronted her when we found her in the woods – Marcus will back me up – and she didn't seem to know what I was talking about. Can't stand the woman, but I think she was telling the truth. I know when she's lying, and I don't think she was."

"So who else feels strongly enough about you to want to vandalise your room?" asked Lindsay, thinking that this case was getting interesting and could lead to a promotion for her and Andy, if they played their cards right.

"No-one that I can think of," said Max. There was no way he was going to tell them about the girl with the teeth and Vibrant Waters, and he certainly wasn't going to mention the unfortunate incident with Pamela on the first night.

"Shall we take a look at the room?" said Andy.

Max led the way. At the door, Lindsay said, "Thank you sir, that'll be fine. We'll take it from here." Clearly dismissed, Max headed back to the seminar room. He hadn't got around to telling the police about the latest happening, and as they hadn't asked about the girl, he assumed that they didn't yet know that Tessa was the second person to go missing in the short time that they'd all been together.

The two constables looked around the room.

"Someone likes playing with toothpaste," said Andy.

"It's pretty superficial," said Lindsay. "It looks like whoever did it was in a hurry – there's not much cut up, just these cigarettes."

"Almost like a kid," said Andy.

"Maybe it was a kid," said Lindsay, stooping to pick something up from the carpet. "Whoever it was liked chocolate buttons."

Andy went to look at the chocolate button held gingerly in Lindsay's latex-gloved hand.

"Aye, that's a Cadbury's chocolate button, right enough," he said, holding out an evidence bag for his colleague.

"Writers, eh?" said Lindsay.

"Just have to hope this lot aren't poets," said Andy.

Chapter 19

It took Tessa some seconds to adjust to the gloom inside Malcolm's hallway. There was a dank smell about the place that she hadn't expected. Somehow she'd pictured him living in a light, airy flat or cottage with cheery neighbours nearby; yet here they were in this squat little bungalow, a mile or two out of the village. How easy it would be to find yourself snowed in. She shivered.

"This way," said Malcolm, and she hopped after him, leaning heavily on the crutches, and through the farthest door. It led into a sitting room that looked as if it hadn't been sat in for a decade. The surfaces were dull and dusty. Everything looked old. The windows were opaque with ancient grime, and cobwebs dangled from the picture rail. No way was this a young man's home.

"Who lives here?" asked Tessa. "Surely this isn't your house?"

"It's my mother's," said Malcolm. "I just have to check something, and then I want to show you my collection."

Tessa was suddenly afraid. Fear pulsed, toxic, icy and liquid through her entire being.

"We'll talk to the students now," Andy MacLeod said to Marcus. "Do you have a list?"

Marcus produced the guest list and handed it to the constable.

"We'll start with Dee Brannigan," said Andy. "By the way, do you know who's got a liking for Cadbury's chocolate buttons?"

"No, I can't say I do," said Marcus. He went to fetch Dee, and saw, for the first time, the ghoulish set piece on the table – on the Skye Creative Hub's beautiful Victorian polished oak table. "What the hell's going on in here?" he shouted. "Who's done this to my table? And look at my carpet! Look what you've done!"

Beryl stood and went over to Marcus. "We don't know who's done it," she said. "We've been trying to work it out – it wasn't any of us, and we don't see how it could have been Tessa."

"Christ!" said Marcus, "Jesus Christ! I mean, how am I going to explain this to the Hub's owners? Oh shit."

"We're about to clear it up," said Dee.

"You're wanted by the polis," said Marcus. "They want to talk to everyone, and you're first. Get off to the library."

Dee was pleased to get out of the room. Anything was better than putting up with the atmosphere in there, even being interviewed by the police. She doubted if there was anything useful she could tell them, anyway.

"Are you looking for Anna Meredith too?" asked Dee, after she'd told Andy and Lindsay everything she knew about Tessa's disappearance, which amounted to very little.

"Who is Anna Meredith?" asked Lindsay.

"One of the students. She vanished after the first evening," said Dee. "We think she decided the course wasn't for her and caught the next ferry to Mallaig. It's just that some of us thought you should have been told, seeing as no-one's heard from her."

"I think we need to find out more about this," said Andy. "What else can you tell us?"

"Not a lot," said Dee. "She was quiet, liked Stephen King, that's about it."

"Stephen King? The horror writer?" said Lindsay.

"That's right," said Dee.

"I see," said Lindsay. "Thank you. We'll be in touch if we want to ask you anything else."

Dee couldn't face going back to the seminar room. She'd take her laptop and sit in the rose garden for a while, see if she could make some progress with her book. If Lou didn't resort to cutting herself, what would she do? What options did she have? She went upstairs to her bedroom to fetch the laptop. Something caught her eye, and she turned to the window. It was fast and fleeting, but she was sure she'd seen someone vanish into the shrubbery.

"So this is your mother's house," said Tessa, trying to keep her voice even and hide her terror.

"It *was* my mother's house," corrected Malcolm. "It's mine now. She left it to me."

"But you don't live here?"

"No, I don't live here. Too many memories. Not all of them good memories at that."

"Well, it's very interesting, but I wonder if we could go to the house that you live in? I'm dying for a cup of tea."

"All in good time," said Malcolm. "I have to show you my collection first."

"Your collection of what?" asked Tessa, knowing as she asked the question that she dreaded hearing the answer.

"You'll see," said Malcolm.

Beryl had come clean with the constables. They'd been sympathetic, and agreed to say nothing to the others.

"Did you notice anything about Tessa Birnie's behaviour?" asked Lindsay.

"I can't say that I did," said Beryl. "She's very driven to complete her own book, and she didn't seem to be one to socialise with us all that much. I can't say that I rate her knowledge of English literature, or her sense of what's good, for that matter." She explained about the extract she'd given Tessa to read. "I'd have expected her to recognise it," she said, "but she didn't."

"How would you describe the relationship between Ms Birnie and Mr Logan?" asked Lindsay.

"Fractious," said Beryl. "They seemed incapable of exchanging a civil word. They really are most unprofessional. Very disappointing."

"Did you notice Mr Logan's movements this morning?"

"He was down for breakfast. He and Marcus went to look for Tessa, but he didn't go back when Marcus took the wheelchair down. Leon and Leila went with Marcus. I'm not sure where Max Logan went. He said he was going to change rooms. I didn't see him leave the building."

"Thank you," said Andy. "We'll be in touch."

Megan slipped on her coat and went down to the studio. It was a cedar wood outbuilding that they used for the fine arts groups. They rarely opened it up for the writing groups, as there was plenty of room in the main house for the tutorials and seminars. No-one would think of looking for her there, and she could tidy it up a bit in readiness for the pottery group due to arrive next week, and then return to the house once the police had gone. Members of this group probably didn't know it existed. She'd picked up the key from the key cupboard in the hall, but when she reached the studio, she found, to her surprise, that the door was already unlocked.

Chapter 20

Under normal circumstances, Tessa would have legged it. She was lean and fit and she ran at least five miles most days. Just her luck to find herself in the house out of *Psycho* with an unhinged postman and a badly sprained ankle. She could, of course, turn her crutches into weapons, knock him unconscious, hobble out of the house, and hope for a passing motorist. Maybe one would pass before the sun went down, before Malcolm regained consciousness. She didn't hold out much hope, though. If Max were here, he'd think of something: he was ingenious at concocting plots, and he'd got his protagonists out of worse fixes than this. But Max was probably celebrating her disappearance and thinking about how to seduce Leila Morris. There was no way on earth he'd find her at this place. No, she'd have to rely on her wits. Try to outsmart him. He was probably deluded, psychotic, or else he had some kind of personality disorder that required her to make him think he was in control. She'd need to play along until her chance for escape arose. Strange that she hadn't picked up anything untoward. Strange that he seemed so at home with the doctor, and with Hazel the receptionist.

Malcolm led her to a dusty sofa and went to help her to sit.

"I'm happier standing for now," said Tessa, knowing that she'd never get up unaided from that sofa with its long dead stuffing.

"No, you've got to sit. Rest that ankle," insisted Malcolm, starting to take her crutches.

"I'm fine," said Tessa, getting ready to swing. "I don't need to sit down. Thank you," she added.

"Oh, but your ankle," said Malcolm, moving again as if to take the crutches.

Everything that Tessa had ever learnt in every martial art in which she'd dabbled came rushing back. Raising the knee of her bad leg, she jabbed it into Malcolm's crotch, causing him to double up in pain. Balancing on the other leg, she brought one of the crutches crashing down onto the back of his head. Malcolm crumpled into unconsciousness, and Tessa swung her body as fast as she could towards that green, flaky front door. Soon she was outside, the soft afternoon light dazzling her after the gloom of the house. Hopping on the good leg, and using her crutches to propel her body forwards, she swung down the lane, not daring to look back.

Megan wondered who could have opened the studio door. She and Marcus always kept it locked in case of travellers or passing thieves. Not that crime was a problem on Skye. They had their fair share of motoring offences, a few domestics and arrests for drunkenness, but the community was largely peaceable and the tourists who visited came for the quiet and the countryside. Megan opened the door.

"Hello?" she called. There was no reply. She could smell soap, and the scent of a recently peeled orange; yet they hadn't hosted a fine arts group for at least a fortnight. Megan turned on the light. The tables wore their usual fine coating of dust, usually red or grey from the ceramic workshops; but she noticed a clean patch along the working surface near the sink, and looking down, she saw footprints on the dusty floor. On one of the tables there was an empty packet of Cadbury's chocolate buttons.

Ok, that was it: first thing tomorrow she'd be off. This place was too creepy for words. Her boyfriend would be happy for her to go and stay with him – he'd been asking her to move in for weeks. She'd go up to his house after dinner, and then she'd tell Marcus that she quit. He wouldn't be very happy, but it was tough. She stepped back towards the door and out of the studio. She heard a car driving off, and thought it must be the polis. Good, it would be safe for her to go back into the house.

Leon had told the police all that he knew which, he thought, amounted to very little. Now they seemed as interested in Anna Meredith as they were in Tessa Birnie, and he too wondered if there was a connection. They'd all been told not to leave the house, and to phone with any additional information that may occur to them.

Pamela trotted after Max as he went to smoke on the terrace. She looked around to make sure they wouldn't be overheard.

"I didn't tell them, Maxi," she said.

"Tell them what?" asked Max, annoyed that his few moments of peace were yet again being interrupted by this ungainly female.

"About us!" whispered Pamela.

"What about us?" asked Max.

"You know, you looking for me, and coming to make love with me."

"Oh that," said Max. "Well that was a mistake."

"No it wasn't," said Pamela. "You were just overcome by passion. I know there's probably a rule somewhere about tutors not becoming lovers with students, but sometimes you just have to follow your heart. Especially when you're an artist, like we are."

"I wasn't overcome by passion, Pamela," said Max. "I went to the wrong room. Sorry, but there it is. End of."

Pamela looked so hurt that he wished he'd kept his mouth shut and let her have her little illusion.

"You're a lovely lady, don't get me wrong," he said. "But I was …sleepwalking. " He sneezed. Her perfume was causing him to feel as if he was suffocating. "And I should never have compromised you in that way," he added.

She looked at him as if she almost believed him. The thing was, whether he knew it or not, he really did need her, only he just didn't realise it.

"Marcus, someone's been using the studio," Megan said, after she'd closed the door to the office.

"We tell them they can go anywhere, what's the problem?" asked Marcus, who was still relieved that the polis hadn't delved too deeply into his past.

"I don't think it's one of the group," said Megan. "I'd be surprised if they even know it's there. And we always keep it locked."

"You found it open?"

"Yes. There was a smell of food, footprints, remains of a snack. They'd left a chocolate button bag on the table."

At this, Marcus started to pay attention. What was it about chocolate buttons? Hadn't that constable asked him if he'd noticed anyone with a particular liking for them? "Chocolate buttons, you say?"

"There was an empty packet," said Megan. "What did the polis say?"

"They spoke to everyone. I didn't mention you. They might come back and need to talk to you later.

"Were they worried? I mean, did they think something had happened to Ms Birnie?"

"They didn't say. They looked at Max's room, and they were interested in Anna Meredith's disappearance."

"We should go and talk to Angus. We've been saying we would," said Megan.

"You're right. At least we'd know if she'd left the island. Are you happy to take care of dinner?"

"It's easy enough tonight – lasagne. I can cope."

"Do a veggie one for Dee, then."

"They can all have veggie tonight."

"What do you reckon?" Andy MacLeod asked his partner as they drove away from the Skye Creative Hub.

"Not sure," said Lindsay Lennox. "There might be a simple explanation – Anna Meredith decided it wasn't for her and hurried off home, and Tessa Birnie was rescued by someone; but then again, there could be something very sinister going on: why didn't Anna tell anyone she was going, and why is Tessa still missing?"

"Writers, eh?" said Andy.

"The worst," agreed Lindsay.

Chapter 21

Marcus drove to the ferry station thinking about what Megan had said about the studio. Something wasn't right. He was more rattled than he'd let on about Tessa's disappearance, because it didn't seem possible that she'd got herself out of those woods. And if, somehow, someone had come along and got her out before he and the students got back, how come they hadn't brought her back to the house? He'd feel better once he had confirmation that Anna Meredith had left Skye, and Angus was the man to ask.

"Good day, Angus!" called Marcus, as he walked towards the pier. He could see the MV Coruisk crossing the narrow channel from Mallaig. The crossing was a mere twenty-five minutes, so he'd get straight to the point with Angus.

"I'm wanting to pick your brain," said Marcus to the young man in the smart, Caledonian MacBrayne uniform. "Do you remember who took the boat across to the mainland on Sunday?"

"Aye," said Angus. "Weather was fair and we ran almost exactly to time – the boat in was two minutes late, and there was a thirty second delay on the return journey."

"And were there many passengers?" pursued Marcus.

"Eighteen," replied Angus.

"Was there a wee lassie with long fair hair, teeth that stuck out, thin, say five four?"

"No," said Angus. "There was Mrs MacBride, Mr and Mrs Lowther, Miss Francis...."

"You're sure you didn't see anyone you didn't know?"

"Only the Farradays, they were tourists, stayed up at Portree for a week."

"Thank you," said Marcus. Angus was known to have a photographic memory, and his knowledge about boats, ferries, and steam trains of the world was encyclopaedic. He'd been a strange boy, never one to have many friends, but the job he'd landed at Caledonian MacBrayne suited him perfectly. As far as Marcus was concerned, if Angus hadn't seen Anna Meredith, she hadn't been on the ferry. That meant she was either still on the island, or she'd left by going the long way round and going by road over the Skye Bridge. He didn't know how to start checking out whether she'd made that journey. He'd have to leave it to the police now.

Tessa was getting tired, and she stopped at the end of the lane where the houses began. She must be safe now. There was a pub a little way ahead, so she headed towards it; but then she had a terrifying thought: what if there was some kind of conspiracy? She'd heard about the kinds of things that happened in small, isolated communities. Suppose whoever was in the pub was in cahoots with Malcolm, and conspired to give her up to him? There was a bus shelter with a seat inside. She hopped in and sat down, taking care not to put any weight on the still painful ankle. Had she not gone into the shelter at that particular moment, she would have been visible to Marcus, who was driving back to the Creative Hub from his meeting with Angus, and he would have been mightily relieved to have found one of the missing guests, and she would soon have been sitting comfortably in the warm house. Instead, Tessa took shelter inside the solid little structure, and Marcus drove on by.

"D'you mind if I take a couple of hours off?" said Megan, when Marcus returned. "Lasagne's all ready, I've made some salad, there's cake for dessert."

"No, you go, hen," said Marcus. She'd been going out with her boyfriend for just a few weeks, and he remembered what that was like:

yearning to see each other at every opportunity, and lots of sex. He felt wistful for Edinburgh when he thought about it, but knew that he needed to bide his time, despite his earlier thoughts about abandoning the Creative Hub and going back to face the music in his native city.

"You'll be back tonight?" he said, as Megan buttoned up her coat.

"I'll be back in time to do breakfast, is that ok?" she said, pulling a striped woollen hat over her head.

"Go on, then," said Marcus.

Megan took her bike from the rack around the side of the house. She didn't have far to go. It was downhill from the Creative Hub, and she was outside the little house in the village in fifteen minutes. She was looking forward to a cosy evening with her wonderful new man. He should be in by now, she thought as she knocked on the door. But there was no reply, and she was pretty sure he wouldn't be sleeping. There was only one other place he was likely to be at this time of the day, so she got back on her bike and cycled through the village, and out along the lane towards the hills. It had rained earlier, and everything had a fresh, newly washed feel. The mountains looked misty and golden. A soft breeze tousled the wayside hedgerows. Megan smiled as she pedalled.

Max had led the afternoon sessions, tackling criminal mindsets and how to integrate forensic science into the plot. Ros had not at first thought that this was of any use to her at all; but as Max presented various real life case studies, she realised that this was exactly what she needed, if she were to dispose of Alastair efficiently and without being detected.

"Never underestimate the usefulness of alcohol," said Max. "Not only does it make it a lot easier to manipulate the victim into risky situations, but it will almost always seem that the death was accidental, and caused by the victim's own carelessness. Even better if they're a smoker."

"Like you?" said Leila.

Max laughed nervously. "Yes, like me. If anyone was really out to kill me, the most obvious thing to do would be to get me drunk, add some drugs for potency, and then have me light up a cigarette just before passing out, preferably on a bed or foam mattress." He'd have to be careful, he thought. Suppose it was one of these people who had trashed his room?"

Ros didn't say anything, because she was busy processing these new ideas. Alcohol seemed to offer a wide range of possibilities: she could get him drunk, and then stick a lit cigarette in his mouth, go out and let fire and inflammable furniture do the rest; only he'd given up smoking over two years ago, so that might look suspicious. And it was her home too: she liked it, and planned to stay in it after Alastair's demise. Maybe something with a candle? Or a nasty accident with something flammable from his workshop: he did so love his solvents and gases when we was pottering with his model-making, and he did that in the garage rather than the main house. Yes, this session was definitely proving worthwhile. What if she could get him drunk on the journey home, create an argument at a motorway service station so that he went off without her – for she was certainly not intending to die with him – and then met his death on the motorway? Only problem with that was the likelihood that there would be other victims, and Ros was quite clear that the only person she wished dead was Alastair. She didn't even want Lana to die – just to have acquired a nasty sexually transmitted infection that lingered and mutated and led to permanent pain, infertility, and the utter death of libido.

"Then of course there's always the leg of lamb approach," said Max.

"Poisoned Sunday roast?" asked Pamela, "a bit obvious, I'd have thought."

"Not poisoned," said Max. "Batter the victim over the head with the frozen joint, making sure the meat's well wrapped in cling-film. Once they're dead, remove the plastic, dispose of it making sure no-one can find it, and cook the joint."

"Oh, I like it," said Pamela. "Do you think you could do it with one of those reconstituted meat things that they grill in kebab shops? Croydon's full of them. Kebab shops, that is."

"Quite possibly," said Max, thinking that he really shouldn't be giving her any more ideas.

"Stabbing your victim with an icicle's pretty classic," said Jack.

"How does that work?" asked Dee, thinking it sounded like the kind of revenge action that might appeal to Lou.

"Stab your victim with an icicle through the eye," said Jack, then put it somewhere where it'll melt. No weapon, you see. The perfect murder."

Ros was tempted, but the thought of poking something through Alastair's eye was just too gruesome. What if his eyeball fluid squirted out, or there were bits of brain on the icicle? No, that one wasn't for her.

Leon was intrigued, but he found Max's approach far too earth bound and conventional. It was about time, he thought, that they got some younger people teaching these programmes. People who were clued up about sci fi and fantasy, steampunk, the sorts of things that most people wanted to read about these days. Major Gonzales would never resort to anything so underhand, anyway: his mission was to do good and to eradicate evil. And the Deathorians were more likely to use biological warfare or toxify the oceans by turning them radioactive.

Beryl was rather impressed at the way Max had prepared for the session, and it was clear that he'd stimulated the imaginations of the students. She rather wished she'd thought about the icicle when she'd been writing *Dear Departed*.

"Dinner will be ready in half an hour," said Marcus, as the session was coming to a close. The students headed towards the bedrooms, all going towards the stairs, except for Jack, who accessed his annex through the French windows.

As Max passed the door to Tessa's room, he found himself wishing she'd turn up. Where on earth could she be? She'd been gone now for most of the day. If it was some kind of joke, or her way of getting back at him because he'd laughed at her, then she'd had the effect she desired, and needed to come back. Max decided not to go to his room, but to seek out Marcus to find out if he'd had any more information.

"Heard any more about Tessa?" he said, trying to sound casual.

"No, not a thing," said Marcus. "I expect the police will be asking at the hospital on the mainland. That's the only thing I can think of: someone came by and took her off, and she hasn't been able to let us know because she didn't have her mobile." It was thin, Marcus knew: surely Tessa would have used someone else's phone, or even a call box; but he felt that he needed to do what he could to reassure Max.

Megan reached the house and went to knock on the door. To her surprise, it was already open. She went in, calling as she went. She was used to the gloomy entrance, by now. She hoped someone would buy the bungalow soon and do it up: it needed complete refurbishment, and then it would be a lovely wee home.

"Malcolm?" she called, and then gasped as she walked into the sitting room. "Malcolm! What on earth's happened?" she said, running to tend to her boyfriend who was lying on the sofa looking pale, sick, and dazed.

Chapter 22

"Thank God you're here, Megan," said Malcolm. "There was this crazy woman. I tried to help, but she attacked me. Kneed me in the nuts, Megan, then battered me with her crutches. Honestly, people nowadays…"

"Don't try to speak. I'll call Dr Mackintosh right now," said Megan, reaching into her coat pocket for her mobile.

"Bugger! No signal," she said. "Is the landline working?"

"No, I had it cut off after Mother died," said Malcolm. "I'll be ok, I just need some paracetemol."

"I'll away to the surgery," said Megan. "Will you be ok for five minutes?"

"I think so," said Malcolm, feebly. What was the world coming to, he wondered, when you did everything you could to help someone and by way of repayment they assaulted your manhood and knocked you unconscious with a crutch? He'd been brought up to be a good citizen. He could have just left that woman in the woods, but no, he had to play the hero and try to rescue her. Well, he thought: never again. No more mister nice guy.

Megan got back on her bike and cycled back to the village, peddling as fast as she could. She hoped she'd reach the surgery before it closed. She was in luck: three people sat in reception waiting to see Dr Mackintosh. Hazel McLure was tidying up and getting ready to close for the evening.

"Mrs McLure, it's Malcolm," said Megan.

"Hello there Megan," said Hazel, peering over the top of her reading glasses. "What's the matter then?"

"Someone's attacked him," said Megan, still breathless after her rush from Malcolm's mother's house to the surgery. "I think he's concussed."

"Oh dearie me, whatever next," said Hazel, who blamed the Skye Bridge for all the crime on the island. It was just too easy for all these crazies from the mainland to get to Skye – and get off again evading justice. "Can you get him along here?"

"I don't want to move him," said Megan. "Could Dr Mackintosh come to the house? His mother's house?"

"It'll be after surgery," said Hazel, "But I'll make sure he comes along."

"Thank you," said Megan. "I'll get along back to him."

"You do that," said Hazel. The girl had been going out with Malcolm for the past month or so, but she came from Glasgow or somewhere unsavoury on the mainland. Who was to say it wasn't her who attacked the young man?

Tessa decided to risk going into the pub. She had to get back to the Creative Hub. She was cold and exhausted, and the day had been hellish from the moment she set out for her run. She was surprised that no-one had been sent out to look for her. But then who would have guessed that she'd been abducted on a postie's bike, bundled into a barely roadworthy Fiesta, and then hustled into a psychopath's dead mother's bungalow. She hauled herself up onto the crutches and stood on the edge of the pavement, checking that the road was safe to cross. Just as she was about to step out, a girl on a bicycle hurtled around the corner and had to swerve to miss her.

"Ms Birnie?" The rider had dismounted and now turned to stare.

"Megan," said Tessa. "I'm glad to see you! Can you help me to get back to the house?"

"What happened to you?" asked Megan, shocked to see the usually neat and elegant Ms Birnie bent over a pair of crutches, her hair dull and matted with some kind of debris, her running outfit stained and torn.

"Long story," said Tessa. "I fell, I thought this man was trying to help me, but he wasn't. I managed to get away, now I need to get home."

"You!" cried Megan, "It was you attacked my Malcolm! Well I'm calling the polis and getting them to arrest you."

"Megan, you've got the wrong…"

"Oh no, don't you try to talk your way out of it. I know about folk like you. Think you can get away with hurting a decent, kind man. Well you cannae!"

And before Tessa could interject, Megan had swung herself back onto her bike and was heading for the pub, where there was a public telephone that actually worked. Tessa didn't know whether to follow Megan and try to explain, or whether to hop back into the bus shelter. She decided to carry on towards the pub, and propelled herself across the road. Megan was talking animatedly to whoever was on the other end of the phone. As Tessa walked in, she looked up.

"Aye, she's here now," she said. "That's right, Tessa Birnie. Thanks. Cheers." As she replaced the receiver, she pointed at Tessa as she looked at the barman.

"This is the one," she said. "This is the mad cow who attacked my Malcolm."

The barman lifted the counter and came around. "Best lock the door, then," he said, and lowered the catch on the front door. "Can't have you running off, now, can we?" he said.

"What the fuck's going on?" yelled Tessa, now frantic with pain and confusion. "Just call me a taxi. I need to get back to the Creative Hub. I'm a writer. Tessa Birnie, maybe you've read my books?"

"Never heard of you, darling;" said the barman. "But Malcolm, he's a mate of mine, and I don't like to hear of him being hurt, you get what I'm saying?"

"But he's the one who attacked me!" cried Tessa. "He kidnapped me. Took me to some derelict house, said he had a collection to show me. God knows what he was planning to do!"

The barman looked at Megan, and Megan looked back at him. Suddenly they both began to laugh.

"Malcolm was going to show you his collection?" said Megan.

"God knows what he was going to do!" cried Tessa, thinking that everyone on this island was stark raving mad.

"Did ye no see his collection, then?" asked the barman.

"What collection?" asked Tessa. "I don't believe there was a collection. It was all just a ruse."

"There's a collection, all right," said the barman, and burst out laughing again.

"I've got to run," said Megan. "I left him there, and the doctor will be up soon. He's not in a good way. The polis'll be here for her." Throwing one more accusing glare at Tessa, she unlatched the door and slipped out.

"Please get me back to the house," said Tessa.

"Cannae do that," said the barman. "Got to wait for the cops."

"Well then at least give me a drink," said Tessa, sinking onto a chair. "And tell me where the toilet is. I've been dying to go for hours."

Dr Mackintosh was not a happy man. He seldom was. But he was more convinced than ever that the Skye Creative Hub was the devil's work. Here was a decent local boy in a state of concussion – not life-threatening, he was glad to find – because some hysterical writer had taken it upon herself to assault him with a crutch. And with a crutch that he, Dr Mackintosh, had issued to her only that afternoon. How she could have behaved so wickedly after all that boy had done for her, he couldn't fathom. Well, at least young Megan seemed decent enough.

"You'll feel better in the morning," said Dr Mackintosh. "Now, can you get yourself home?"

"Aye, I think I could get back now," said Malcolm. Seeing Megan had worked wonders. They only had to go the length of the village.

"Come and see me tomorrow evening," said Dr Mackintosh, "and call me straight away if you start to feel ill or vomit."

"I'll stay with him," said Megan.

"Just you make sure he rests," said the doctor. "There'll be time enough for the other stuff when he's better."

Megan felt the colour rise in her face, but she nodded her agreement to the silver-haired man who was old enough to be her grandfather.

"Shall we go?" she said to Malcolm, and the two prepared to follow Dr Mackintosh out of the funny little bungalow.

"I only came here to show her my collection," said Malcolm. "I thought she seemed nice. Thought she'd be interested."

"Her loss," said Megan, closing the door behind them.

Andy Macleod picked up the call during the constables' lunch break. They'd stopped at a nice little pub near Broadford.

"So we're going back?" said Lindsay Lennox, a touch of weariness in her voice: it had been a long day and she wanted to get home to feed the dog and put her feet up.

"Afraid so," said Andy. "Alleged assault, we may need to make an arrest."

"But how did she get there?"

"Who knows? But we're about to find out."

The barman relented. Where was the harm in showing the woman the toilet? No way she was going to escape out of that wee window. Tessa was relieved as she sat to pee. She thought about locking the door and staying in the toilet until Max or someone civilised came to rescue her. But she was thirsty, too, and the barman had promised her a drink. She flushed and went to wash her hands. Glancing in the mirror, she was shocked at her image: wild, dishevelled, dirty: thank goodness Zak wasn't around to see her like this. What would he say about it all? She couldn't think of any suitable Zak-type platitudes. She washed her face and dried it as best she could with the roller towel. Back in the bar, she sat back in the chair she'd been occupying.

"What'll ye have?" said the barman.

Tessa was torn between whisky and a large mug of tea. "Whisky and a glass of water please," she said.

"Just a single, mind," said the barman, pulling the amber liquid from the optic and then pouring a glass of water from the tap underneath the bar. He walked them over to Tessa's table, taking care not to get closer than he needed to: she clearly couldn't be trusted with those crutches.

Tessa drank down the whisky and felt its warmth soothe her.
"I need to ring the Creative Centre," she said.

"Phone's over there," said the barman.

"I don't have any money," said Tessa.

"How are you planning to pay for that dram?" asked the
barman

"Well…I thought…given the circumstances…it would be on
the house," said Tessa.

"Don't know where you got that idea," said the barman, "but
I'll no be paying for your phone call on top. I've a living to make here,
you know."

"Could you ring them from the pub phone?" asked Tessa.
People in London, she thought to herself, were so much more friendly
and helpful than these backwoods Scots.

"Cops will ring them for ye," said the barman. He switched on
the large television and turned away from Tessa as the screen filled
with a football match.

Chapter 23

She thought about turning his new room over, but it felt too unoriginal. She didn't want him getting used to a particular form of disruption. What if he became blasé about it? *Oh, hi guys, someone's trashed my room again. Anyone got a light?* No, she needed to turn up the heat. She could leave the dead bird she saw in the shrubbery in his bed. He'd get a nasty shock when he went to settle down for the night. Or something with more blood and wetness: but she'd have to find something to kill, and there wasn't any obvious prey. She'd noticed a black and white cat skulking around, but it never went near the house and she guessed it was either feral or lived elsewhere. And she'd never killed a cat. And then she thought about a more subtle approach which might achieve her aims rather more dramatically. She'd need to be stealthy, and she'd need to be prepared to exit as soon as she'd done it, and there was a chance she'd be caught: yes, it was risky, but worth it. And she'd use the dead bird too.

Andy MacLeod and Lindsay Lennox were sitting in Malcolm's cosy sitting room. He was sporting a nasty bruise on his head and there was still a trace of blood around his chin.

"Is this where it happened?" asked Lindsay.

"No, I'd taken her to my mother's bungalow," said Malcolm. "It's away up the road."

"We'll need to take a look," said Andy.

"I can take you," said Megan. "You'll be all right on your own while I go, won't you?" she said to Malcolm.

"If you're sure," said Malcolm.

Andy and Lindsay indicated that they were happy for Megan to show them the site of the assault. They left Malcolm nursing a cup of tea.

"Where's Tessa Birnie now?" asked Lindsay as they all got into the police car.

"I left her at the pub with Rob," said Megan

"We'll go there after we've seen the house," said Andy.

Tessa wondered how much longer she'd have to wait. The barman was wholly absorbed in the football game that was being played out by the Old Firm. She'd long finished her whisky, and he'd made it clear that there was no more unless she had the means to pay for it. She thought about trying to escape as customers entered and left

the bar, but she couldn't move quickly enough, and she definitely

couldn't walk all the way to the Creative Hub. She'd just have to wait

for the police to come, and then she'd be able to explain about being

abducted and held against her will. And then they'd take her home.

Zak would say something upbeat: *Well think of it this way, Tessa: if*

you'd twisted your ankle in London, you'd have spent the day in A and

E at an NHS hospital in meltdown. At least this way you've had fresh

air and met some new people. Zak encouraged her to take the glass half

full approach. *There are two types of Scrabble players in the world,*

he'd once said, *those who see Z and Q as opportunities, and those who*

see them as the worst letters you can pick out. Tessa liked to see

herself as a Scrabble optimist, but as far as her current situation went,

she was struggling to find anything positive in it at all. Except,

perhaps, the fact that she had escaped Malcolm's collection, and had

evaded a potentially untimely end.

Marcus had served dinner, and the group had sat together,

eating quietly. Everyone was worried now about what could have

happened to Tessa, and no-one was in the mood for casual chat. Dee

helped Marcus to clear the empty dishes away.

"Has this happened before?" she asked, wiping dry a plate.

"No," said Marcus. "Sure we have our share of dramatics, but we've not had people going missing. Never had the polis up at the house."

"And it's really not part of the programme?"

"No, it's for real."

"Tessa couldn't have slipped back down the bank into the stream, could she?"

"We looked. She'd just gone."

Leila brought a half full salad bowl into the kitchen. "No-one's got much appetite," she said. "I think I should call our agent, Tessa's and mine, that is. Can I use the phone?"

"Sure," said Marcus.

Leila rang Dinah Tannenbaum's number. The agent picked up after the fourth ring.

"Leila, darling! How wonderful to hear from you!"

Leila told her about Tessa's disappearance.

"That's very strange," said Dinah. "She just vanished?"

"Yes," said Leila. "No-one's heard from her all day, and we're getting really worried. I think we should let her next of kin know. Do you know who they are?"

"I don't, I'm afraid," said Dinah. "Of course, she *was* married to Max Logan. Toxic relationship. Have you read any of his books? They say that the corpse in *Death in the Mall* was the image – literally speaking – of Tessa."

"He's here too," said Leila. "He's the other tutor."

Leila heard a sharp intake of breath, and then there was a long silence. "Dinah? Are you still there?"

"Yes, yes, I'm here. Look, Leila, where was Max Logan at the time of Tessa's disappearance?"

"He was one of the ones who found her, when she was sitting injured in the woods, but he didn't go back to help her back to the house. Said he didn't want to risk putting his back out – he'd had an accident the night before."

"So could he have slipped back without anyone knowing?"

"He was teaching for most of the morning," said Leila. "He wouldn't have had much time."

"Well, if you ask me, that man has the answer," said Dinah. "Their marriage was famously brutal. It wouldn't surprise me if he'd found a way of getting rid of her."

"He's foul, it's true, but…" said Leila, shuddering as she thought of how Max had started to pursue her, of his lecherous leer. But was he capable of hurting, or killing, his ex-wife?"

"Are the police involved?" asked Dinah

"They're looking for her," said Leila. "We haven't heard anything, though, so I guess they haven't found her yet."

"Make sure they know about Max," said Dinah. "I do know someone who may know how to contact her family, if she has one. I'll make a call. And stay away from Max Logan until all this is sorted out."

After they'd ended the call, Dinah Tannenbaum searched out the number she was looking for. Then she phoned Zak Summers to tell him that he should be very concerned about his lucrative client.

Beryl went to Jack's annex with him. He poured them each a generous measure of the single malt.

"I'll have to go shopping soon!" he said, pointing to the bottle, which was almost empty.

"We'll take some time out tomorrow," said Beryl. "Go to the village. That's if all this mess is sorted out."

"Eh?"

"Have to wait for this mess to unravel," said Beryl, raising her voice.

"D'you think there's been foul play?"

"I'm not sure, Jack. It's very odd that she just disappeared like that. And Anna too. We all seem to be forgetting about her in our panic about Tessa. But I'm not convinced that she ever left."

"Why?"

"Just a feeling."

They sipped at their whisky, and took stock of the strange and disturbing day.

"Max's session was good, I'll give him that," said Beryl, after a while.

"He knows his stuff. Did you read *Blood in the Mall*?"

"I did. It wasn't up there with Rendell and James, but he kept you guessing until the end. Nice use of forensic science. Application of DNA was ingenious."

"So if he wanted to commit a crime and get away with it, he'd know how to do it."

"He would. But I'm not convinced he's the type."

Night had fallen and the clear sky was twinkling with stars. The moon was big and bright. The air was cool and fragrant.

"You staying?" asked Jack.

"Yes," said Beryl. "Mind you don't snore."

Jack laughed. "I'm too deaf to notice whether *you* snore or not!"

"Perfect," said Beryl. "I brought my toothbrush."

Leila, Dee , and Leon decided to stay up to critically appraise each others' work. They huddled in the library, a bottle of red wine in the centre of the table.

"I still think they might be testing us," said Leon. "You know, making strange things happen and seeing how we react, as writers.

"I don't think so," said Leila. "Tessa was really hurt: she couldn't have faked that ankle."

"Marcus insisted that this wasn't some kind of game to get us all plotting. I'm still wondering what happened to Anna," said Dee.

"What if Max has done something to Tessa?" said Leila, thinking back to her conversation with Dinah.

"They hate each other," said Dee.

"That doesn't mean he'd hurt her," said Leon. "Not *all* men are violent."

"They all have the potential to be," said Dee.

"And women don't?" said Leon.

"I think we should stay away from him," said Leila. "Until we know."

"But he couldn't," said Leon. "He was here, with us."

"Yeah, that's true, but what if he ran back down during one of his smoking breaks, did her in, raced back in time for our next session?"

"Max Logan? Racing? Get real!" said Leon. And although she didn't say anything, Leila was inclined to agree.

Max was weary. It had been a long, tough day. Not knowing what had happened to Tessa was almost worse than having to put up with her nasty presence. And then there was the wretched, omnipresent Pamela, and trying to shake her off was no joke. He didn't want to give up on Leila – once Tessa was back and things had got back to normal, he'd offer her some one to one help with her book. She'd soon come round and fall for his charms, they always did. Well, almost always. Not so often these days, if he was honest. He went to the kitchen to see if there was any drink lying around. He needed something sweet and strong, and if he couldn't have Leila, whisky would have to do instead. Marcus was writing out a menu.

"Heard anything?" asked Max.

"Not a thing," said Marcus.

"Worth putting in a call to the police, don't you think?"

"They would have called us, I'm sure; but I'll try them just in case. Never had much faith in the polis, and they usually post the dead losses of the force on the islands."

"Any chance of a drink?"

Marcus reached into the cupboard for the Talisker. "One of those days," he said, pouring Max a generous measure, and then doing the same for himself. "I'll go and call the polis," he said and went to the office. Lindsay Lennox had left a card with their number on it. He dialled. Max hovered by the door.

"It's Marcus Dean, Skye Creative Hub," said Marcus. "I just wondered...you have? Where? She what? You're going to what? Is that necessary? I see. Aye, I know....aye, I'll tell them. Goodnight."

"What was that about?" asked Max.

Marcus stroked his chin and shook his head in disbelief. "You'll not credit it," he said.

"What?"

"They've arrested her. They're taking her to the cells."

"Tessa?"

"Aye, Tessa Birnie."

"What do you mean? What's that stupid woman done?" He was so relieved to hear she was alive, he began to be angry with her all over again. Things could go back to normal. Almost.

"She's charged with assaulting our postie," said Marcus.

Max burst out laughing. "Assaulting a postie! Whatever next!"

"It's no funny," said Marcus, indignantly. "He's a fine young man, is Malcolm. Wouldnae harm a fly, let alone a woman."

"We'll have to tell people," said Max. "Let them know she's ok."

"Aye, but she isnae all right," said Marcus. "She's heading for the cells with that nasty ankle."

"You think we should go…"

"Well, I think *I* should. I'm paid to take care of folk while they're here."

"Now?"

"After we've told everyone."

"I suppose I'd better come with you. Nearest thing to next of kin."

Marcus found the little trio in the library and shared his news.

"Assaulting a postman?" cried Leon. Maybe the woman did have balls after all. And he'd been right about women being potentially violent too. Sort those bloody feminists out!

Max was surprised to find Beryl in Jack's room, for it was she who answered the door, and she had toothpaste around her mouth. Well, at least someone was getting lucky. Or maybe not, he thought, wondering what Jack could see in the old woman – or what she'd see in him. Mind you, he'd choose Beryl over Pamela any day, despite the tweedy skirts and sensible shoes. Although of course, he'd choose neither if Leila stopped playing hard to get.

"She's not been hurt, then?" Beryl was saying.

"No more than she was when we last saw her," said Max, "as far as we know. I'll go with Marcus to try to bail her."

"Good. Now we'll all sleep," said Beryl.

Ros and Pamela were in the computer room, working on their books. Ros had started a new one. For the first time, she was writing a contemporary story, and a crime story at that. Pamela was testing some plot ideas that had to do with a new shopping centre – yet another – being built in Croydon, and the unearthing of bones which may turn out to be human.

"Oh thank God," said Pamela on hearing the news. "You must be relieved, hun, what with her being your ex and all that."

"You're going to get her now?" said Ros.

"With Marcus," said Max.

"You drive carefully," said Pamela. "Make sure you take your phone and put a couple of blankets in the car."

Insufferable, thought Max.

Marcus and Max climbed into the Skye Creative Hub minibus. It would be a long drive to Portree, which was where the police had taken Tessa. They'd be lucky to be back by dawn. Yet both set off with lighter hearts than they'd had earlier that day.

She had prepared everything, put her bag where she could easily collect it and make her swift departure. She wished she'd been brave enough to go to the village shop to buy some more chocolate buttons. She'd only got a few left. She'd eke them out. The dead bird was in his washbasin. As a bonus, she'd found an outsized spider, and she'd placed that in the shower tray. The windows were open, and the room was already chilly. Now she just had to wait. Had Max not moved rooms, she would have heard the minibus engine start up and she would have turned to see the two men leave the Hub. But she was in the quiet room facing the garden, and she heard nothing. She waited.

Chapter 24

"You say you didn't assault Mr Craig, Ms Birnie?" Andy MacLeod was interviewing Tessa, and Lindsay Lennox was taking notes.

"I acted in self-defence," said Tessa. "He'd abducted me, taken me to this dank, dilapidated cottage. The way he was talking about his collection, I felt sure he was going to harm me."

"But he didn't physically attack you?"

"No, no he didn't touch me. Only to help me up, and get me in and out of his car, that sort of thing."

"So he was being helpful?"

"Well, I thought he was, but then this dreadful house…and his collection…"

"Did you actually see his collection?"

"No, I escaped before he was able to do anything."

"And you don't think your assault on him was unprovoked?"

"No! He was threatening me."

"How exactly?"

"Well, all this talk about the collection. And that house. It was his dead mother's. You *have* seen *Psycho*, haven't you?"

Max and Marcus didn't talk much as they drove up the island. Max was wondering what kind of state Tessa would be in, and Marcus was hoping that no-one who knew him had been posted to Skye from Edinburgh. It wasn't hard to find the police station once they reached Portree. Somerled Square was just off the main road.

"Will I wait here for you while you fetch her?" asked Marcus. He was relieved when Max agreed.

Max walked into the police station. "I've come for Tessa Birnie," he said to the sergeant on duty behind the desk.

"There she is," said the sergeant, nodding towards the area behind Max. He had to look twice. There was only one woman in the waiting area, and it was Tessa; but he'd never, even in the worst days of their marriage, seen her look so desperate and dirty. A pair of crutches lolled behind her, and the sprained ankle, despite its strapping, looked even more swollen than it had that morning. He felt a pang of something in his belly. It was a strange feeling, not one he was used to experiencing, or certainly not in relation to Tessa. He thought it might be pity.

"Prince Charming to the rescue," he said.

Tessa looked up at her ex-husband with something close to affection. "I didn't think anyone would come," she said.

"Couldn't leave you here," Max said. "I'd have had to run the rest of the course by myself, and you're bloody well not getting away with dumping that on me."

""Just get me out of here," said Tessa with a sniff.

"Are you free to go?"

"Tell you about it in the car." She rose with difficulty and reached for her crutches.

"Has anyone looked at that ankle?"

"Dr Mackintosh did, earlier on. He didn't do much, just strapped it and gave me pills. I lost them at the mad postie's house. It hurts like hell."

"There was a sign to a hospital. We'd better stop by. Tell you what, you've a great plot for a story."

The Portree Community Hospital was a couple of minutes away, and the accident and emergency department was still open. Max helped Tessa out of the minibus and into the harsh glare of the hospital strip lights.

"You're lucky it's a Monday," said the triage nurse. "Not many people drink on a Monday. Not to excess, anyway. We'll soon get you seen."

Tessa sat in the waiting area, her injured ankle resting on a chair in front of her.

"So tell me, one time light of my life," said Max, "just how did you manage to pull off your little vanishing act? You know they've been whispering about my having done away with you."

Tessa told him about Malcolm the postie and his bike, and getting a lift into the village and seeing the doctor.

"It was all going fine until he took me to his mother's house," she said. "It was like the house in *Psycho*, you know, where the dead mother's still sitting in her chair, and Norman Bates kills the girl in the shower."

"He kills her in the motel," said Max. "The shower's in the motel room."

"I know, but he was going on about showing me his collection, and we were miles from anywhere, and I thought he was going to rape me and then kill me."

Max bit back an uncharitable comment about needing to be desperate, and Tessa's current unattractive state. "So you finally put all that kung fu to some good use?" he said.

"Tae Kwondo," she said. "Yes. Rather well, it seems."

"Rather *too* well if they're charging you with assault."

"He's not pressing charges," said Tessa. "For some reason, part way through their grilling of me, they stopped, while someone brought in a message. Apparently it said that he wasn't going to press charges."

"You know he's that girl Megan's boyfriend?"

"Megan from the Hub?"

"The same."

"Oh," said Tessa. "So maybe she talked him out of it. I think she likes my books."

"Or maybe he's just a decent man who doesn't want the hassle," said Max.

"Well he needs to learn not to take vulnerable women to his own personal house of horrors!" said Tessa. "I mean, what does he expect?"

"The doctor will see you now," said the nurse. Tessa hopped along behind her into a cubicle.

Tessa's x-ray showed there was no fracture. The doctor re-strapped her ankle, gave her strict instructions to keep it elevated, chastised her for not putting ice on it straight away, and sent her off with a pocket full of painkillers.

Marcus started up the engine of the minibus, and the three of them drove back in silence. Tessa fell asleep, stretched out on the back seat. Max covered her with a rug. He was wondering how to run the rest of the week, because he couldn't see Tessa functioning at her usual level. Actually, it would be a lot easier if he could just get on and finish the course, despite what he'd said to her earlier. No more arguments or having to negotiate with the wretched woman. Yes, he could see advantages. Marcus was thinking he'd had a lucky break, having such close encounters with the polis, but still managing to maintain his conveniently low profile.

They arrived back at the house some time after two, but well ahead of the time they'd thought it might take. Tessa was groggy from her deep sleep, and cold, in the way that you always are after a long journey through the night. She fumbled with the crutches.

"I'll help you up," said Max.

"Thank you," said Tessa, for once glad that he'd been there.

"I've got the room next to you," said Max. "If you need anything, just yell. Right, I'm off for a fag."

Tessa shut the door behind her and sank onto her bed. She desperately needed a shower, but she was too exhausted: it would have to wait until the morning. She stripped off her clothes, slipped a nightshirt over her head, and headed for the bathroom. A pee, a cursory wash, a clean of her teeth, and she limped back towards the big bed and fell back onto it, pulling the covers over herself and falling asleep almost instantly.

She'd waited an hour. And then another. There were no more chocolate buttons. She felt her legs grow heavy and her eyes start to close. Where was he? She looked out of the window. There'd been no movement out there for an hour or so, after that elderly couple had gone into the annex. The house was quiet. There'd been footsteps on the stairs earlier, the flushing of distant toilets, the opening and closing of doors; but there'd been no sound other than the soughing of trees for an hour, or maybe two. She would hear him come in, that was for sure. She could afford to curl herself up on the floor behind the curtains. She'd wake as he approached the room, and then she'd spring into action.

Max savoured his cigarette. What a day. What a night, come to think of it. But no further harm had come to him, and Tessa was back safe. He still wondered what had happened to the girl with the teeth. Anyway, the police had her details: if anything had happened to her they'd have found out by now. And he hadn't needed to answer any awkward questions. But Max didn't believe his own reassurance. He knew all too well, from his research for his books, that people did disappear, and often it was years before they were found, and sometimes they remained lost forever. Look at Fred and Rosemary West: they killed scores of women, and weren't caught for decades. Some of the women they're thought to have killed have never been found. So anything could have happened to Anna. He hoped she had simply gone home, and that there wouldn't be any further complications. Now, how was he going to move things on with luscious Leila? Maybe Tessa's indisposition could work in his favour. He stubbed out the cigarette and went back into the house. He locked the French windows behind him – Marcus had asked him to do so if he went for a late smoke. The house was quiet, seemingly peaceful. Max went into the kitchen and switched on the light. He'd have another drop of Marcus's whisky. He swigged from the bottle, then turned out the light and headed for his room. The stairs creaked as he ascended, but otherwise there was no sound. He entered his bedroom and shivered. He didn't remember leaving all the windows open, but the curtains were blowing and the room was icy. He needed a shower, but decided to go straight to bed: the dramas of the day, and being nice to Tessa had exhausted him. He undressed and threw his clothes in a pile on the chair. He thought about cleaning his teeth and decided not to bother. He couldn't even be arsed to close the windows – some fresh air would do him good, and the bedding was almost too warm. Naked, he slipped between the sheets. He'd forgotten to lock the door, couldn't remember where he'd put the key, but it was too bad. In seconds he was asleep and snoring loudly.

Beryl and Jack were sound asleep in a companionable spoon arrangement. Earlier, Beryl had been reading a novel by her second favourite Indian writer, Rohinton Mistry.

"Who's your favourite then?" asked Jack.

"Vikram Seth. *A Suitable Boy* has to be one of the most perfect novels ever written. Not that Tessa Birnie would recognise fine literature if it leapt off the page and smacked her."

Jack was enjoying the new Ian Rankin.

"Is there life after Rebus?" asked Beryl.

"Looks like it," said Jack.

"Jack," said Beryl.

"Mm?"

"What will you say to your wife?"

"What about?"

"About this. Us."

"Don't think I'll say anything," he said. "Why? D'you think I should?"

Pamela had heard the minibus return. Thank heavens, she'd thought to herself. Max was back, safe and sound. Peeping around her curtains, she'd watched Max help Tessa into the house. She'd heard the creak of the stairs as they made their way to their bedrooms, and she'd heard one door open and close, and then footsteps head downstairs. He'd be going for his cigarette. It wasn't long before she heard him come up again, his door opening and closing softly. She'd give him time to undress and wash, to get himself comfortably into bed, and then she'd go and give him the comfort she was sure that he would need after such an arduous day.

Leon woke in a cold sweat. Jesus Christ! What the fuck was going on? He could just about accept Major Gonzales cross-dressing, especially if he was going undercover and it was all in the best interests of the overall mission; but in his dream tonight, what Major Gonzales had been doing to Marcus Dean was utterly out of character, and Leon was mightily disturbed. Having gone to a public school, not much surprised Leon about what boys and men did to and with each other; but Mother had always warned him about bullies and big boys, and on the whole, apart from a rather nasty phase in the third year, he'd managed to keep himself to himself. Yes, that was a pretty apt way of describing it. He'd found there was a knack to making oneself invisible, and he'd perfected it. He'd spent his teen years waiting to escape the school and evolve into the strong and fearless man that he knew was the real Leon Waterson. He saw his boyhood self as a chrysalis, a feeble persona that masked his true, fierce self. In reality, Major Gonzales and he were one and the same, which is why this latest twist in his rather active dream life was so bizarre and disturbing.

This was not how it was meant to be. She cursed herself for having fallen asleep and having to hide herself in a hurry. Then she cursed him for his slovenly ways and lack of personal hygiene. Things were not going to plan, and that made her feel very angry indeed.

Chapter 25

It had been a long hard drive, and Alastair was relieved to see the lights of the Skye Bridge looming ahead. He'd thought about taking the car ferry from Mallaig, but the ferry times were few and far between and he decided he'd arrive quicker if he went across the bridge. None of this *over the seas to Skye* romantic tosh that his wife had been so excited about.

His wife. He had to sort things out with her, persuade her that she'd leapt to the wrong conclusion, and that nothing was endangering their marriage. Lana had been annoyed when he'd told her he was heading up to Scotland, and needed to make the journey alone. He'd said it was something to do with a distant member of the family and helping them to settle a legal problem, but he didn't think he'd fooled Lana.

"I'm starting to feel like the other woman," she'd said to him. He hadn't liked to tell her that she was, in fact, the other woman. And that was how he planned to keep it. No reason to upset the status quo. It suited him to be living with Ros in their nice mock Tudor detached house in Walton on Thames. The golf course was within easy reach, and he enjoyed passing the time with the other chaps at the local pub and sometimes on the river itself. He and Ros rubbed along all right. She understood his needs, and he was generous to her. This trip to Scotland was a case in point: he'd paid for several for her this year. Why not? It was good for her to have a creative outlet, especially as they hadn't managed to have children. Shame that. He'd have liked to have had a kid or two, a boy to carry on the family name, a girl who'd look up to him and tell him he was the best daddy in the world. But it hadn't happened. He thought Ros would have been a different person if she'd had children: fulfilled, and not always feeling the odd one out when all her women friends were producing babies like they'd gone out of fashion, and her sisters too. He'd seen the auntie act start to wear thin. She'd spent years trying to persuade anyone who questioned her childlessness that it was infinitely preferable to be an auntie, to let others ruin their pelvic floors in giving birth and grow haggard through sleepless nights. As an auntie, she could have all of the pleasure and very little of the pain. But as the nieces and nephews grew into their teens and drifted away, the mantra began to lose its power. *I think we need some pain to make the pleasure feel more special,* she'd once said to him, after her youngest sister's second child had swanned off to university.

That had been several years ago. Now they lived companionably enough together, but when Lana had arrived at work as the new secretary, he had recognised in a dazzling flash what he was missing in his life. She was gorgeous, but didn't quite know it. And she willingly accepted his invitations to discuss their cases over a glass of wine in the local wine bar. He'd listened to her tales about the unfaithful boyfriend, and if she'd seen his attention as being somewhat avuncular at the beginning, things had changed when they'd gone to Nottingham to represent a particularly complex case that had required two overnight stays in a Holiday Inn.

Ros's writing courses had provided him with opportunities to further his relationship with Lana, and he'd seen it as a win-win situation: Ros always came home happy and energised, and she found him to be most attentive and loving, glad to see a glimpse of the cheerful, sexy man she'd married.

But now the proverbial shit had hit the manically whirring fan, and it was up to him to get it all sorted out, limiting the damage as far as he possibly could. He'd started out early that morning, driven into the night, fuelling his journey with black coffee and motorway service station junk food. His only hope was that she'd be so pleased to see him, and so convinced of his sincerity, that she'd drop these silly notions of divorce.

Pamela slipped along the corridor, trying to avoid the creaky floor boards. She failed, and her footsteps told out loud the story of her mission to minister to Max. She felt a chill draft as she approached his door, and was struck by the arctic feel of the room as she crept in. Silly man must have left his windows open! She'd soon sort that out. The moon was bright, the curtains blowing into the room revealing a starry night. She could discern his huddled shape in the bed. She tiptoed across to the window to close it. And then Pamela screamed. She screamed with her whole, huge, petrified being. She unleashed an unearthly, off-scale, eardrum-shattering scream that caused Max to wake with a terrified start, and the rest of the house to wonder who had been killed. And as Max's sleep-heavy eyes adjusted to the moonlit gloom, he watched a ghostly figure brandishing something sharp and glinting flit across the room and vanish out of the door. Pamela clutched at her chest and sank to the floor, her translucent nightdress splayed around her, giving an impression of a beached jellyfish. *What the fuck?* Thought Max. Suddenly someone flung open his door and switched on the light. Tessa stood there, looking grey, leaning on her crutches.

"Oh Jesus, Max," she said, as she took in the chaotic scene, windows flung wide open, curtains blowing like angry sprites, Pamela large and senseless on the floor.

"It's not what it seems," said Max. "I don't know how she got here."

"You must be desperate," said Tessa, leaning her crutches against the chair so as to crouch down and check whether Pamela was breathing.

"What's she doing here?" asked Max.

"You don't know?"

"I didn't ask her, that's for sure."

"Was she waiting for you when you got to bed?"

"I don't know. Don't think so. I just crashed."

Pamela was stirring and started to moan. "Oh Maxi," she said, "why didn't you warn me about the ghost?" and then she seemed to lose consciousness again.

"I'll get a cold towel to put on her head," said Tessa, hobbling to the bathroom. "Why don't you put some clothes on?" She pulled on the light cord and then screamed.

"Fuck Max! Fuck! Oh Jesus, that's so gross…"

"What now?" Max felt increasingly that he was immersed in some surreal nightmare from which he'd soon awaken. A bit like Leon and his daft character, Major whatever. This couldn't be real. Still naked, he followed Tessa to the bathroom. She was pointing at the basin, and he saw, with disgust, what it was that had shocked her. He was a seasoned thriller writer, his research took him into all sorts of gruesome forensic reports; but he was appalled at the sight of the dead bird, the slit cavity of its breast alive with maggots, in his sink. "How the fuck did that get there?"

"You didn't put it there?"

"Of course I bloody didn't."

"Christ, Max, look at the size of that spider!" There, crouched on the tiled wall of the shower cubicle, was the largest spider that Max had ever seen. It was Amazonian in its size and menace. And he knew that there would be nothing he could do about it. For it was a little known fact that Max Logan suffered from acute arachnophobia.

Pamela came out of her swoon to find Tessa patting her hand.

"Come on Pamela, time to wake up," she said, as if Pamela was some infant who'd dozed off.

"Did you see it?" said Pamela.

"See what?"

"The ghost. It was here."

"You saw a ghost?" Pamela could tell by Tessa's tone that she didn't believe her; but she knew what she'd seen.

"It was behind the curtains," she said. "Lunged out as I went to shut the window."

"What were you doing here in the first place?"

"There's no need to talk to me like that," said Pamela. "I wanted to check that Max was all right after his long drive. I thought it was simply wonderful of him to go to your rescue after you'd been arrested."

"You didn't think to knock? Or maybe to wait until the morning?"

"It's ok Tessa," said Max, "leave her to come round. I think there was someone else. I saw them flash by as I woke up."

"I told you there was a ghost," said Pamela.

"I don't think it was a ghost," said Max, pulling on his trousers.

"But it came from behind the curtains," said Pamela, who had struggled into a sitting position, "and it was so thin. Ethereal. What else could it have been?"

Max was sure that another person had been in his room. He wondered if it had been Leila Morris, whether Leila had come to him as he'd been sure she would, only Pamela had frightened her off. He'd have to have a quiet word tomorrow. Encourage her to come back, let her know that he hadn't invited Pamela in. But would Leila have been wielding a knife?

Dee had been woken by Pamela's sharp cry. She pulled a sweatshirt over her purple and green pyjamas, the lovely satin pair that Nuala had bought her last Christmas. *Suffragette jimjams!* She'd said, as Dee had unwrapped the plump parcel. She put on her slippers – for Dee never felt quite dressed enough without something on her feet – and padded down the corridor towards the light and a buzz of voices.

To her surprise, and embarrassment, the commotion was coming from Max's room, and lying on the floor in a puddle of silky negligee was Pamela. Dee was no prude, but she felt shocked to find her fellow student in such a compromised position; and her opinion of Max Logan sank lower than it had been before. There were things that shouldn't happen between tutors and students. She believed in maintaining appropriate boundaries. And besides, how could he be so obvious over his lust for Leila (which Dee quite understood: if it wasn't for Nuala, she'd be pursuing Leila herself) and then invite Pamela into his room at night. It was disgusting. And he'd obviously hurt her, she didn't look at all well. Bastard! Just like all men. It didn't occur to her that Pamela might have invited herself. Tessa Birnie was there too, patting at Pamela's hand. "Can't you keep the noise down?" Dee asked.

"Bit of a crisis," said Tessa, "but would you mind making a cup of tea for Pamela and Max?"

"I don't need fucking tea," growled Max. "Get me that bottle of Talisker that Marcus has for emergencies."

Dee headed for the stairs. She couldn't very well say no, but she was well pissed off. She liked her sleep and didn't take kindly to being disturbed. She was surprised to find the kitchen light on and the back door open. Who'd be so careless as to leave it wide open on such a cold night? She called outside, in case someone had gone for a cigarette or to gaze at the stars. No-one answered, so she pulled the door shut and turned the key to lock it. She didn't notice the blade that glinted in the moonlight on the path that led to the studio. Then she set about making tea, banging the mugs down on the working surface with feeling. She'd have to tell Nuala about this. She'd go into the village to use the call box tomorrow, that was for sure. She was already missing her partner with her quick smile, haywire curls, and sharp mind. Nothing like a little time apart to appreciate what was waiting at home. And being with this strange group certainly made Dee appreciate her life back in Bristol.

Leon sat up in bed. He'd been jolted out of his sleep by Pamela's scream. Marcus Dean had been fiercely fucking Major Gonzales. He was almost grateful for the rude awakening. Gonzales would never allow that to happen, he'd have killed Marcus rather than have him do those things to him. But Leon was more turned on than he could remember being. No way could he get up and investigate what was happening outside.

Ros heard the racket and sighed. This course was proving to be far from restful and conducive to creativity. She hadn't been asleep. Her mind had been hyperactive with thoughts of Alastair and what she'd do about his treachery. Was she really cut out to be a murderess? Even if she was able to get away with it? Probably not, let's face it. So she'd need to find a shit hot lawyer to screw him for every penny she could. She thought she knew just the person – had met him at the golf club a couple of months ago. Probably more sensible than risking prison. She'd never been overly fond of the close company of other women. The noise outside died down. Probably Pamela trying to seduce Max again, she thought. She wouldn't bother to go out to find out.

Marcus heard a piercing scream followed by the muffled sounds of activity in the house from his bedsit in the attic. He'd been watching late night porn on a cable channel. He pressed the pause button. God, this group was the worst to date. Worse even than the poets that had come last summer, and he hadn't thought that was possible. No, the sooner he could pack up his things and move back to Edinburgh, the better. Or maybe he'd try Glasgow for a change of scene. Not too many people knew him there. He waited to see if the noise would die down. The scream was a one-off, but he could tell that there was still activity. He supposed he'd better go down and investigate. But on second thoughts, they knew where to find him, they were all adults. He went back to his movie. Firefighters getting it on. Big, butch firefighters, muscles rippling, faces streaked with grime from the fire they'd just subdued. You could almost smell the sweat.

Pamela's scream had woken Leila, too. God! She was hating this retreat. It was a real nightmare, and certainly wasn't helping her to finish her novel. She'd tell Dinah Tannenbaum what to do with her ideas when she got back to London. It wasn't even as if there was anything happening that would give her inspiration for her next novel. It was all way too banal, and her fellow students were amateurish bores. Still she'd better see what was happening. She wrapped a striped dressing gown around her Monsoon nightdress and stood outside her bedroom door to ascertain where the sound was coming from. It sounded as if something was happening in Anna's old room, the one that Max had taken over. She went to investigate. Seeing Pamela, that dreadful, coarse woman from Croydon with her clichéd book and plastic jewellery, sprawled out on Max Logan's floor initially filled her with disgust; but then she saw the funny side and burst out laughing.

"What's so funny?" said Max.

"You and Pamela!" shrieked Leila. "God! You must have given her a really good time for her to make all that noise," and Leila doubled up with laughter.

"Grow up," said Tessa. "If you can't do anything useful then fuck off back to bed."

"And that's how you talk to your students?" said Leila, suddenly looking serious. "Well, that'll be something to tell Dinah when I get back."

"Judging by the standard of the work you've brought here, I'd say your days of being in favour with Dinah Tannenbaum are limited," said Tessa.

"Bitch," said Leila, "just because you're a has-been and no-one ever reads your books any more. And you can't even teach!" She turned away before Tessa could muster a response and went back into her bedroom, slamming the door behind her. That was it. She'd head back to Muswell Hill tomorrow morning, and insist that Dinah reimburse her for the money she'd wasted in coming to this sub-standard travesty of a writing programme.

Tessa limped over to the windows to close them, for the room felt freezing. As she drew shut the window and pulled the curtains together, she noticed something on the floor. It was a purple plastic bag that had once contained a comforting measure of chocolate buttons. Max had never liked chocolate, but clearly someone had been here who did.

"I'd like you to go back to your room now," Max said to Pamela. There was something he needed to say, and he could only say it to Tessa.

"I'm not sure I'm well enough…"

"I think you are," said Max. "You'll feel much better back in your nice warm room. Won't she Tessa?"

"Oh yes," said Tessa. "I'll help you back if you like."

"No, that's all right," said Pamela, rising from the floor. "Are you sure you don't need me to stay, Maxi?"

"No Pamela. I didn't need you to come, and I certainly don't need you to stay."

240

"Well you don't have to be like that," pouted Pamela. "I was just trying to help."

"You can help by going now," said Max.

"Well, as long as you're sure," said Pamela. "You know where I am if…"

"Yes, thank you," said Max, his anxiety about the monster in the bathroom growing by the second. At last she was gone, and he was alone in his still cold room with his ex-wife.

"Who's doing all this?" he asked. He was sure now that it couldn't be Tessa.

"Well, Pamela seemed to have invited herself in," said Tessa.

"I don't mean Pamela. I mean the bird, the trashed room, the other person in here tonight."

"Leila?"

"I'm beginning to wonder."

"Not likely to be any of the others. The oldies are busy having it off with each other; Ros is plotting to kill her husband; Leon's struggling with his alter-ego, and Pamela's got the hots for you."

"What about the girl who works with Marcus?"

"Megan? No, she's tending to that homicidal postman, God help her," said Tessa.

"Only it seems he wasn't homicidal…"

"So they say."

"Tess, I can't do it."

"Do what?"

"Go into the bathroom. With that spider. Could you…"

"You want me to go into that bathroom with the dead bird and look for a genetically enhanced spider?"

"I did help you out, old girl."

Tessa remembered similar scenes throughout their marriage. He came across all suave alpha-male until faced with a creature that had eight legs. And then he was transformed into something altogether opposite. Catapulted back to scared little boy. She'd used it against him before now. Called him stupid and sissy. Right now she didn't have the heart to. And much as she loathed spiders, she was capable of catching them and relocating them to their natural habitat if she needed to.

"You'll have to deal with the bird," she said, "and the maggots."

242

"And you'll relocate Frankenstein?"

"It was the monster that was the problem, not Dr F."

"You'll get rid of the spider?"

"If you help me up."

"Look Tess, this whole thing's got me a bit rattled, and this room's freezing. I don't suppose…"

"What?"

"You've got that big bed…"

"You're asking to share my room?"

"Just for tonight. It won't kill you."

Tessa sighed. She looked around the shambles of this room, his second in two days, and almost as wrecked as the first, "No, I don't suppose it will," she said.

Finally the house settled back into slumber. Even Ros drifted off, and Max and Tessa lay as far apart from each other as was possible in the king-sized bed, the dead bird and its maggots having been bundled into a plastic bag and relocated to the bin outside, and the oversized arachnid having been tossed vigorously out of the window so that it could return to its woodland home. Marcus remained ignorant of the details of the evening's drama and went to sleep fantasising about naked fire-fighters finding ingenious things to do with hoses.

She'd escaped out of the back door without being seen. That dreadful woman in her frightful nightwear wouldn't have recognised her and she didn't think Max Logan had seen her either. He'd seen enough to know that someone had been in his room, and he'd find the second little tableau she'd set up soon enough. Good, they'd be nicely spooked, which is how she wanted it, even though things were far from perfect: the woman coming in had ruined her plan. She'd had to abandon the best part, and she cursed the fat woman from Croydon. She'd have to complete her revenge another time. It wasn't safe for her to stay in the studio any more. That girl Megan had been snooping around, and she'd probably be back in the morning. She'd need to go first thing in the morning, take the morning ferry. She wondered if her community psychiatric nurse had noticed that she'd missed a couple of appointments. They'd look for her before long, she wasn't supposed to go away without telling them. She just had one final thing to do before her work here was finished and she could return. Then she'd turn up for Wednesday's appointment as if nothing had happened.

Chapter 26

Alastair didn't see the lorry coming. His eyes must have closed for a second, maybe two, and suddenly there was the deep blare of truck horns, rapid and dazzling flashes of light, and the headlights were coming for him. He tried to swerve, but it was too late. It seemed as if he and the car stopped still for a moment, then he felt himself propelled backwards and the last thing he knew was the feeling of life being crushed out of him and the explosion of metal on metal.

"Aren't we due a day off?" said Lindsay Lennox when she answered Andy's call.

"Aye, but we've got to see to this one first."

"Nasty?"

"Not much left of the BMW driver by all accounts."

"And the lorry driver?"

"Broken ribs. He was lucky. Pays to be in the cab, you're higher up. Mind you, if it turns out it's his fault, he'll have to face up to having killed someone."

"See you there?"

"Aye."

The first thing Tessa wanted to do was to have a shower. Her sleep had revitalised her, and she wanted to scrub the fear and filth of yesterday away. Max was still asleep, snoring softly. She was surprised at how normal it seemed to have him in her bed. She had to remind herself of his philandering ways and unpleasant habits as she hobbled to the shower. She was still very stiff but the ankle was less painful. She unwound the bandage and turned on the shower.

Max awoke to the sound of running water. He stretched out and wondered for a moment how he'd come to be in this luxuriously large bed. Then he remembered. He got up and shuffled to the bathroom where Tessa was soaping herself in the shower. He lifted the toilet seat.

"Hey!" shouted Tessa. "Wait until I'm out!"

But he was already peeing. That was another thing she'd hated about living with him. Still it could have been worse, he might have needed a dump, and her being in the shower wouldn't have stopped him. She scrubbed herself harder as she remembered showers overshadowed by the sound and smell of Max shitting.

Bloody woman! He thought. *Everyone pees, why does she have to be so precious about it? And what about her nasty dental floss habit?* He'd go back to the room next door to shower and dress, and just hope that nothing else had happened during his absence.

Ros woke still feeling rough, but having made a decision. She would tell Alastair that he could have the house in France as long as she could stay in their Walton on Thames home. That seemed fair enough. And she wanted to start proceedings straight away. She'd ask Marcus to use the office phone – after all, it was something of an emergency.

When Leon went down for breakfast, the first person he saw was Marcus, who was laying out the cereals and jams. Leon noticed Marcus's tight bottom, slim legs, and long-fingered, delicate hands.

"Morning Leon," said Marcus. "Sleep well?"

"Morning," said Leon, and noticed for perhaps the first time how beautiful were Marcus's eyes. So blue they were almost violet.

Oh, and that suggestion of fine chest hair peeping out of the open neck of his shirt. Leon was aware of his pulse racing faster. *Oh my God!* He thought, *this can't be happening!*

"Toast?" said Marcus, wondering why the boy was staring at him. "Oh…yes… please," said Leon.

"Everything all right?" said Marcus. "You're looking a wee bit peely wally."

"I'm fine," said Leon, aiming to sound more like Major Gonzales than like a tongue-tied fourth former. "Why wouldn't I be? I'm straight… I mean, I'm fine. Just fine. Let me help you with that," and he grabbed the bowl of muesli and placed it manfully on the table.

Leila had packed her case. She brought it downstairs and parked it in the office. "Marcus?" she called.

"Seeing to breakfast," Marcus called back. "I'll be with you in a jiffy." He finished setting out the plates and cutlery. When he went into the office, Leila Morris was tapping her foot with impatience. She'd tied her long wavy hair back, which made her look more adult. The frown on her face detracted from her prettiness.

"I need you to book me a cab," she said. "I want to catch the morning ferry."

"I'll run you down," said Marcus. "Going to the mainland for the day?"

"No, I'm leaving," said Leila. "Isn't it obvious, with my case down here?"

"The course isn't finished yet," said Marcus. "Why do you want to go now?"

"Do you really have to ask?"

"No need to be rude."

"It's been a disaster from the beginning. Neither of those two inept tutors can teach – God knows how they got picked to run programmes here. Seems to me that all anyone's interested in is getting into someone else's bed, and frankly that's not what I paid for."

"I'm sorry you feel like that," said Marcus. "Isn't there anything I can do to change your mind?"

"No, just let me catch that boat so that I'm on my way home in good time," she said.

Marcus heard the back door opening and Megan's voice calling.

"Hey Marcus, I'm here," she said.

"Ok, that's good," he said. Then, turning to Leila, "So you want me to take you now? You wouldn't rather say goodbye to Ms Birnie and Mr Logan?"

"No, I don't think there's any need for that."

"Suit yourself," said Marcus, thinking that one disgruntled resident fewer would be no bad thing. "I'll just go and tell Megan."

He went into the kitchen, where Megan was taking off her outdoor clothes. "You missed quite a night," he said. "But we've got Tessa Birnie back."

"That woman! I'll kill her!" said Megan. "D'you know what she did to my Malcolm?"

"I heard," said Marcus.

"I told him, I said, you *should* press charges; but not Malcolm, no: she's probably got problems, he said. I'll not press charges, he said. We'll just let the matter rest, that's what he said. Well, wait until *I* see her: she'll have a piece of my mind, right enough!"

"She's a guest, Megan, and it's between the polis and Malcolm and her now. Stay out of it, that's my advice."

"Well, I don't know how you expect me to stay civil, serve up her food, do stuff for her. Not after this, Marcus. I'm human too, you know."

"I know that Megan."

"And I want to quit," she added. "This place creeps me out. I'll give you a week's notice, Marcus," she said, "but I'll no be sleeping here. I'll stay with Malcolm and be here for breakfast, but there's too much weirdness going on. And what if that girl Anna's dead and buried somewhere in the grounds? How do we know she's not? I reckon Tessa Birnie's capable of anything."

"Are you finished?"

"Aye. That's all I wanted to say."

"Good. Well, first of all, you're on two weeks' notice, not one week. Second, there's no dead body here at the Hub. The girl must have left the island by the bridge."

"And you know that how?" she said, hands on hips, exasperated beyond belief by his stupid assumptions.

"Trust me, she's not dead," said Marcus. What he didn't say was that he was ninety percent certain that he saw Anna Meredith last night when he was locking up. And he thought he knew who'd been using the studio.

"Do you mind if I use your phone?" asked Ros when she came downstairs. Marcus was putting on his coat, ready to take Leila to the ferry station. He was beyond caring about the Hub's rules about phone use.

"Go ahead," he said. "Try to keep it short."

Ros dialled the number for their house. He wouldn't have left for work yet. It was their Ukranian help, Bella, who answered.

"Yes? This is Lambert household," said Bella.

"Bella, it's me, Mrs Lambert. Is Mr Lambert there?"

"No, Mrs Lambert. Yesterday he leave. He say he take trip to Scotland. You are in Scotland, isn't it?"

"Yes, I am," said Ros. Surely he wouldn't be coming to see her. He must be thumbing his nose at her by taking that harlot Lana north of the border.

"His secretary is in office if you need talk with her," added Bella.

"Is she indeed?" muttered Ros. "Did he say when he'd be returning?"

"No, he leave in hurry. Packed small bag."

"Thank you Bella. Please make sure you clean the tops of the picture frames. See you soon." Ros put the phone down. Then she dialled Alastair's office number. Lana picked up on second ring.

"Is he there?" asked Ros, abruptly.

"No, Mrs Lambert. He's taken a couple of days off to sort out some family business in Scotland. At least, that's what he said."

"Yes of course, I should have remembered," said Ros and hung up. Next she dialled his mobile. Maybe she should have started with that, but he so often had it switched to silent mode. A message told her that the number was not available. She guessed she'd have to wait until either he showed up – which she hoped he wouldn't – or she got home. But in the meantime, she could book an appointment with the hottest divorce lawyer in Walton on Thames.

Leila climbed into the Skye Creative Hub minibus, and Marcus put her case into the luggage space at the back.

"Can I grab a lift?" asked Dee, who'd come running after them. "I need to go into the village."

"Sure," said Marcus, wondering what was more important than breakfast for all these people.

He dropped Dee at the post office, and promised to pick her up on the way back. Then he took Leila to the ferry port.

"I'm sorry you didn't have a better time," he said.

"You can tell Tessa Birnie and Max Logan that I'll be putting in an official complaint," said Leila. "And I'll be writing to *Mslexia* and *Writing Magazine*. People need to know what a sham this place is."

"We do our best," said Marcus. "I'm sorry it didn't live up to your expectations." He handed Leila her case and went to shake her hand. She offered hers reluctantly, and then turned to board the ferry, which was already in.

Leila liked to sit outside on boats and she was looking forward to the short but spectacular crossing with its misty mountain views. She sat herself near the front and looked out across the water. As the boat moved off, she was startled by a voice she had not expected to hear again.

"Hello Leila," said Anna.

Chapter 27

Dee made sure she'd got a purse full of change. Then she went into the Ardvassar Hotel to use the phone. She rang her home telephone number. She was surprised when her best buddy, Nat answered. What was Nat doing in her house? Maybe there was something wrong with Nuala?

"Hi Nat," she said. "Is Nuala there?"

"Oh, hi Dee," said Nat. She sounded odd. Almost nervous, Dee thought. "I'll go and get her."

Dee could hear whispering in the background, and then she heard the familiar soft Irish accent of the woman she loved most in the world. It was time, she thought, that they celebrated their commitment by having a civil partnership.

"Hello Dee," said Nuala. "You're phoning early! Is anything wrong?"

"No," said Dee. "I just wanted to hear your voice, tell you I love you, find out what's going on, you know…"

"Nothing's going on," said Nuala, and Dee knew that it was.

Zak Summers was a canny businessman. He knew how to keep his clients happy. After the call from Dinah Tannenbaum, he tried ringing Tessa's phone. It went straight to voicemail. Dinah had mentioned something about poor mobile coverage, maybe that was it. Dinah had rung him a second time to say that Tessa had been found and was safe, but he didn't know anything else. It was a fair bet that she'd welcome his reassuring, empowering presence, though. She'd mentioned the job at the Skye Creative Hub in one of their life coaching sessions. She'd been pleased, because these residential courses paid well and meant that she didn't have to teach dreary, underpaid evening classes in London. Zak had been delighted, because if his clients were doing well, then so was he, especially if they thought his intervention had a lot to do with their success. They kept coming back for more, and they told their friends about him. He'd googled the Creative Hub, and now he rang the number. The line was busy for a good few minutes, but eventually a woman answered.

"Skye Creative Hub, Megan here," she said.

"Hi," said Zak, "I wondered if I could talk to Tessa Birnie."

"Are you the polis?"

"No, I'm her...I'm a...friend," said Zak, wondering why she might assume he was the police. It sounded ominous.

"I'll see if she's around," said Megan, and laid the receiver on the office desk. She didn't want anything to do with Tessa Birnie, much less to help her out by telling her that someone was phoning her. Still, Marcus was right, it was her job, and she needed her wages.

Tessa was eating breakfast in the dining room.

"Phone for you," said Megan, before turning on her heel.

"Who is it?" asked Tessa.

"I'm not your bloody secretary," Megan called back, "go and find out for yourself."

Tessa was not used to being treated with such hostility. Megan must be unaware of the ordeal to which she had been subjected by the girl's boyfriend. She feared that Megan would find out what he was really like in good time. No doubt he'd be wanting to show her his collection too. She limped into the office and picked up the phone.

"Hello?"

"Darling!" said Zak, "are you all right? I've been hearing worrying tales about you disappearing."

"Zak!" cried Tessa, overjoyed to hear a friendly voice, the voice of someone who was just there for her, at least for ninety minutes once a fortnight. "How did you find me?"

"Synergetic vibes," said Zak. "There's such a strong empathy between us."

"How did you know?"

"I sensed something was awry, and so I spoke with Dinah Tannenbaum, who'd been speaking with one of your students, I believe."

"Leila Morris," said Tessa, who realised she'd yet to encounter Leila that morning. "Yes, it's all been rather awful." She started to tell him about her misadventures, but he interrupted.

"I'm on my way," he said. "Tell all when you see me."

"But you can't," said Tessa, "it's too far…"

"Nowhere's too far for my favourite client," said Zak. "And I sense that you're in urgent need of a session."

"I can come to see you when I'm back in London," said Tessa, worrying about her bank account and those nasty letters about her overdraft. "I'm only here for a few more days." But the truth was that she'd love to see Zak. He'd make everything all right. He'd help her to reframe things, to visualise moving on. She couldn't think of anyone she'd rather see. And she'd completely failed to immerse herself in her own writing, as she'd planned. Zak would help her to get back on track.

"You need to invest in yourself," said Zak. "I'll be with you this evening. You're worth it, Tessa, don't forget that."

Beryl and Jack decided to skip breakfast. Jack had a packet of chocolate digestives secreted in his wardrobe, and he'd brought a cafetiere and some decent coffee. They had breakfast in bed.

"Remember Julie Felix?" said Beryl.

"Wonder what happened to her."

"Did you ever go to *Le Macabre?* In Soho?"

"Read poetry there," said Jack, "awful stuff. Pretentious."

"Weren't we all?"

"At least Foyles is still there."

"And Gaby's. I think she's still touring."

"Who?"

"Julie Felix."

Pamela took time to get herself ready. She felt embarrassed about the events of the previous night, and above all, she felt misunderstood. After all, it had been Max who'd come to *her* room on that first evening. She'd been trying to give him the love and care that he deserved. But now that she knew the house to be haunted, she was having serious doubts about staying. She could take the afternoon ferry back to the mainland, find a nice hotel for a few nights, get on with her book. Maybe she could persuade Max to go with her: he must be under terrible strain, what with all the goings on, and he really shouldn't have to stay in a house that seemed to have something against him.

Marcus thought that Dee looked dejected when he collected her from outside the Ardvassar Hotel. She got back into the minibus without saying anything and huddled in against the door.

"You ok, Dee?"

"Yeah."

"Only you're not looking too bright."

"I'm fine."

Marcus decided not to push it any further. He'd just get her back to the Creative Hub. Whatever was wrong was none of his business. He hoped to have a quiet few minutes in order to write his letter of resignation to the Hub's owners. If Megan left too they'd be pretty stuffed, but that wasn't his problem. Who bothered about their employers' problems these days anyway?

Dee felt thoroughly miserable. Nat had always said she fancied Nuala. Nuala had always claimed that Nat was too tomboy for her tastes. But no sooner was Dee safely out of the way on a Scottish island, than the two of them got together: her lover and her so-called best buddy. Well, she had always known she was worthless. The universe or God or whatever was paying her back for that little deception about the literary prize. And looking at things objectively, it wasn't any wonder, really, that they'd dumped her in order to enjoy each other. How stupid she was to have thought about asking Nuala to be her civil partner. And how naïve to have believed that Nuala thought she had talent, that that was why she was sending her on the course. No, Dee realised. Nuala had just wanted to get her out of the way. It was almost funny: she, Dee Brannigan, and that toffee-nosed Ros were in the same boat. Nuala's timing was shitty: it was only a week before her birthday. Big four-o. Nuala knew she was freaking out about it. So much for love. Now she just wanted to be at the house. She wanted to go up to her room and search out that razor blade that she remembered packing.

Tessa sat at the dining table and cut up an apple. She had missed her morning run, and she couldn't contemplate practising pilates with Max in the room, and she still couldn't put much weight on the injured ankle. By the time Max had gone back to his own room, it had been too late anyway. And then there had been the call from Zak. So now she had to think about how to get the programme back on track. Max was smoking in the garden. She'd have to liaise with him when he came in. No she wouldn't, she'd *tell* him what they were going to do. She thought he'd be pretty amenable after the nocturnal dramas and her generosity in sharing her bed. She wanted to focus on dialogue. Some of the group wrote reasonable dialogue – Jack's wasn't at all bad – but some of them had a lot to learn. Today would be dialogue day.

She wondered when Zak would turn up. She didn't really want him to meet her here – she felt that a separation between the personal and the professional was in order, and she certainly didn't want Zak and Max to coincide. That could be very nasty indeed. But she was far from mobile. She'd ask Marcus if he knew of anywhere more private.

Maybe that studio further down the garden. She didn't think anyone used it.

Ros continued to write her new book in the computer room. She was revelling in writing from experience and subjective feeling, rather than crafting a story around historical facts. Yes, this was utterly liberating. She had just got to the part where the heroine – for so she perceived the jilted wife – was creating a bomb with kitchen and household fluids when Megan came to find her.

"Ros, it's the polis – sorry, the police, to see you," she said.

"Me?"

"Aye, they're asking for you."

Ros was baffled: why would the police want to see her, unless it was to do with yesterday's happenings, and she didn't have anything to say about either Anna's disappearance or Tessa's, which in any case now seemed resolved.

"Should I come down?"

"I've put them in the office, you can talk to them there."

Ros followed Megan downstairs. She recognised the two officers from their visit the day before, but they introduced themselves again for good measure.

"You are Mrs Rosalind Lambert?" said Lindsay Lennox.

"Yes, I am," said Ros. "What's going on?"

"Does your husband own a BMW?"

"Yes, he does." Surely they wouldn't be interrogating her for some traffic light violation or speeding offence he'd committed?

"Is the registration number GU10AJV?"

"I think so. I'm not sure. What's all this about?"

"Mrs Lambert," said Lindsay, "I'm sorry to tell you that there's been a terrible accident."

"What kind of an accident?"

"Mr Lambert's car was involved in an accident just over the Skye Bridge in the early hours," said Andy MacLeod. "I'm afraid he was killed outright."

"But he can't have been!" cried Ros, suddenly filled with a terrible coldness. "I was going to divorce him! He's been having an affair with his secretary, you know."

"Aye, well, it's too late for all that now," said Andy. "I'm afraid your husband, if it was he who was driving the car, didn't stand a chance."

"So it might not have been him?" said Ros.

"I'm afraid we'll need you to help us identify him," said Lindsay.

"Oh no," said Ros, "no, I don't think…"

"We'll make it as easy as we can," said Lindsay. "We'll need to go by dental records, but if you can identify some jewellery he was wearing, that'll be a good start. I'm really sorry, Mrs Lambert."

"You mean, you think he's…"

"It's almost certainly your husband's body," said Andy.

"Oh," said Ros, ashen faced. "Oh. I see."

"Is there anyone we can call?" asked Lindsay. "Your son or daughter perhaps?"

"No," said Ros. "No, there isn't."

Ros got up and left the room. She went back to the computer room and sat down at the computer where she'd been writing her new novel. She'd written ninety-four pages. She pressed the edit button, selected all the text, and then pressed delete. Then she shut down the computer and went back down to the office, where Andy MacLeod and Lindsay Lennox were explaining what had happened and the reason for their visit to Marcus.

"I'm ready now," said Ros. "You can take me to see him."

"Wouldn't you like a cup of tea first?" said Lindsay.

"No. I'd like to go now, please," said Ros.

"Is there someone you'd like to come with you?"

"No. Let's just go. Please."

Chapter 28

Had Dee known about the preparations for her birthday, she wouldn't have thought about cutting. Had she not assumed the worst, she would not have made such a mess in the bathroom. Back in Bristol, Nat and Nuala were deep in conversation:

"D'you think she suspects?"

"Not sure. She sounded surprised that I was here."

"She wouldn't think…"

"No! No offence, Nat, but she knows I don't fancy you."

"But she might…"

"She knows I'm nuts about her. Why would she think anything?"

"It's a bit early for me to have called round."

"Oh well, I'll make up something, sure I will. Now won't she just love her party?"

"I hope so. She's never been one for big parties."

"Yeah, but it's her fortieth. You have to have a party when you're forty. She'd be mad as hell if we didn't do anything!"

"You're right. What did you do with the list?"

But Dee, of course, knew nothing of this and so she slashed at her thigh with the razor blade, slashed until the pain of the cuts succeeded in pushing back the pain in her soul. When she'd finished, she wiped up the blood and stuck some plasters on the cuts. Then she was ready to face the rest of the day.

"Everyone wondered where you were," said Leila.

"Yeah, I bet they looked really hard for me," said Anna, a hard edge to her voice.

"They did, as a matter of fact," said Leila. They even called the police."

Anna blanched at this news. "What did *they* do?" she asked.

"Started to look for you, I s'pose," said Leila. "How come you're still here? What have you been doing? Where did you go?"

"Doesn't matter," said Anna. "You leaving, then?"

"Yeah, I've had enough. All sorts of weird things happening, a lot of them to Max Logan, whom I loathe, by the way. And then we wasted a day looking for Tessa Birnie, only it turns out she'd been charged with assaulting a postman…"

Anna gave a guarded smile. "Fun and games, then?"

"Waste of time and money. But where did you go?"

"Not far. I was never far away."

Leila looked at the girl who'd been her fellow student. There was something odd about her, a coldness of the eyes, a voice that was eerily toneless. Could she have been making mischief if she had never been far away? But why? Leila didn't feel like asking her. It felt too risky.

At last they arrived at the mortuary. Lindsay Lennox helped Ros out of the car and they entered the low, brick building. Ros felt numb. She followed Lindsay as if in a trance.

"We can't show you the body," said the attendant," but I wonder if you'd mind identifying some pieces?"

Ros gasped as the young man produced Alastair's wedding ring and what was left of his watch. And then there was the leather wallet, mangled but still clearly his, the one that she'd given him two Christmases ago, that he placed on his bedside table every night, the one that contained his driving licence and some coins from their last visit to Switzerland.

"Those belong to my husband," whispered Ros. And it hit her suddenly with a punch that carried the force of the universe that Alastair would not be coming back. There'd be no divorce, no reconciliation, no more arguments, no more anniversary dinners at the Oxo Tower, Alastair was gone.

"I think I need to go now," she said to Lindsay.

Chapter 29

Tessa poured another cup of coffee. Max came in from the garden and joined her at the table.

"Feeling better?" he asked.

"Much," said Tessa. "I've been thinking about the outline for today."

"You're not thinking of teaching?"

"Of course I am. That's what I'm here for, and I've only got a sprained ankle. I think we'll focus on dialogue. They could do with the practice."

"I was thinking that point of view would lead on well from yesterday," said Max.

"Dialogue," said Tessa. "That's what I have planned for today."

Back to her old self, then, thought Max. Just when it looked as if things were going to go rather better.

Megan came in from the kitchen.

"Are you not finished yet?" she said. "I need to clear this table." She snatched the mug of coffee from in front of Tessa and strode back out to the kitchen. She had to step neatly to the side to avoid Marcus.

"We've lost Leila Morrison," he said to Max and Tessa.

"How do you mean, lost her?" asked Tessa.

"She's gone. Taken the ferry back to the mainland. Taken her things, said she's going back to London."

Max's spirits sank even lower. With no Leila to brighten up the landscape, it would be a dull and dreary few days. What could have made her leave so suddenly?

"I take it you've heard about Ros Lambert?" continued Marcus.

"Heard what?" said Max.

"Her husband's been killed in a road accident."

"Jesus," said Tessa. "That's awful. Where's Ros?"

"She went to identify what was left," said Marcus. "I don't think she'll be in any shape to continue the course."

"And then there were five..." said Max.

Pamela, Leon, Jack and Beryl assembled for the morning tutorial. Dee joined them after ten minutes. Ros had come back with

Marcus but had gone straight to her room. Tessa had gone to see if she needed anything and to offer condolences.

"I'm so sorry, Ros," she'd said. "Is there anything I can do?"

"No, I'll be quite all right," said Ros. After Tessa left, she sat on her bed and rocked in silence.

Only Beryl and Jack seemed upbeat and ready to enjoy the day. Dee looked pale and withdrawn, more sullen than usual. Leon was chewing at a fingernail and frowning, his mind clearly elsewhere. Even Pamela, normally so ebullient, sat quietly, her colours this morning a rather more muted khaki and gold.

"I'm afraid we had some bad news earlier on," said Tessa.

Max was glad that she'd taken the lead. He hadn't known what to say.

"Oh?" said Beryl, "Not more disappearances? Where are Ros and Leila?"

"Leila's left," said Tessa, "and I'm sorry about that, but the bad news concerns Ros. Her husband's been killed in an accident."

"Oh God!" cried Pamela, " she was going to divorce him! That's if she didn't kill him first! Maybe thoughts really do have wings!"

274

"Just where do you get off, Pamela?" said Dee, lunging from her chair to stand in front of Pamela. "You're the most fucking insensitive person I've ever met. You make me sick."

"That's enough," said Tessa

"No, it isn't," said Dee. "She hasn't an ounce of feeling for anyone else. And I don't much like Ros, but I'm really fucking sorry she's lost her husband like that."

"I'm not staying here to be abused," said Pamela, and walked out. She'd try to get her breath back in the garden, and then she'd ask Megan about the ferry times. This retreat had been disastrous, and she'd never been so insulted. It was cool in the rose garden. Poor Ros, thought Pamela, after a few moments. I'd better go and see if she needs anything.

Back in the seminar room, Beryl broke the silence.

"I think that was rather strong, Dee," she said

"What's that? What did she say?" said Jack

"I said that Dee's contribution was rather strong," said Beryl.

"I missed what she said," said Jack.

"It wasn't very nice," said Beryl.

"Oh, I see," said Jack.

Dee had retreated to her seat and was avoiding eye contact with anyone. She'd have left the room but she didn't want to run into Pamela.

"We're all tense," said Tessa. "Let's take a few minutes to chill."

"Good idea," said Max, who was dying for a smoke. God! All this tension! Why did women always have to make such a drama out of everything?

Leon didn't know what to say or do. So much uncontrolled emotion, and people leaving, and spouses dying violent deaths. Major Gonzales didn't have to deal with all this human mess as he carried out his missions. He rescued people and put worlds to rights and flew between galaxies. Sometimes he stopped to have sex with someone or to re-energise with some Tai Chi. There weren't many tears in Major Gonzales's world, just like there hadn't been in Leon's since that nasty time in the third year. Leon decided that if he'd got trapped in this particular situation, the Major would go and find Marcus and see if the minibus needed its engine tuning or if there was something useful to do like replacing tiles on the roof.

"I'm not in the mood for writing," he said. "Think I'll go and help Marcus."

"Does he need help?" asked Max as he fumbled in his pocket for his Zippo.

"I expect so," said Leon.

"Back in ten," said Tessa.

Jack and Beryl took advantage of some late autumn sunshine and sat near the French windows.

"All very odd," said Jack.

"What is?"

"Girls leaving, people emoting all over the place. I fear it's all too much for the young fellow."

"Leon?"

"Is that his name? Yes, Leon. Of course, he's fallen in love with Marcus, so he probably finds everything else a distraction."

"How can you tell?"

"I've observed, Beryl. When you can't hear most of what's going on, you spend much of your time watching and noticing."

"That's why your characters are always so real."

"Are they? Thank you." And he squeezed her hand.

Marcus was frowning in front of the fuse box in the hall cupboard when Leon found him.

"Problem?" said Major Gonzales

"Aye," said Marcus. "One of the switches keeps tripping. It's the ring main for the ground floor. Have you noticed the lights keep going off?"

"Yes. Problem with the consumer unit?"

"D'you know anything about them?"

"Some"

"Well take a look, see what you think."

Major Gonzales took flight and Leon was left wondering what the consumer unit looked like (he'd read the phrase somewhere) and how he'd be able to tell if anything was wrong.

"Sure," he said. Marcus seemed to be looking at the box with all the fuses, so he stuck his head in the cupboard, frowned, touched some of the switches, flicked a red one on and off, and then came back out to share his findings.

"Doesn't look like the consumer unit," he said. Oh, but Marcus was beautiful! No wonder Major Gonzales…No! Enough of that.

Pamela had left the room before the others, and she headed upstairs to see how Ros was doing. She found Ros still sitting on her bed, rocking back and forth. She didn't say anything as Pamela entered. Pamela felt for Ros. She knew what it was to lose someone. She never talked about it these days, but seeing Ros, brought the old feelings back with a shiver. She sat on the bed next to Ros and put her arm around her. Ros leant into the big woman's shoulder.

"Oh, hun," said Pamela.

Ros gave a little shudder.

The boat docked and the passengers disembarked.

"Where are you going now?" Leila asked Anna.

"Home," said Anna.

"Where's that?"

"Oh, that would be telling. Somewhere south of here. Bye, Leila. Oh, by the way, think of me, if you hear anything about fires on Skye." She gave a smile that was devoid of humour and full of cunning."

"What do you mean?"

"You'll figure it out," said Anna, "bright, attractive woman like you. Of course he wouldn't look twice at me with you in the room. He did once, though." And she was gone. Leila didn't understand how someone could disappear so effectively when the crowd was relatively small; but Anna had managed it. Leila wondered what she'd been talking about. Fire? Could she have done something to the Creative Hub? Leila had had a strong sense of there being something very wrong with Anna Meredith: she seemed cold, detached. Leila had read about people with varying degrees of psychopathy. She'd been researching for a short story she'd written that had done rather well. It seemed to her that Anna ticked all the boxes. Shit. She'd have to warn them at the house.

"What time's the next ferry back?" she asked the Caledonian MacBrayne officer.

"Not until this afternoon," said the portly man. "You're wanting to go back right now?"

"It's urgent," said Leila, "I've...forgotten something. I need to get back."

"Quickest way is over the bridge," said the man.

"But I don't have a car."

"Angus!" called the man, "Got room for another one?"

Marcus knew that the boy didn't have a clue, but he humoured him nonetheless. He was pretty enough, and seemed to want to help.

"Is there a problem with the electrics?" said Megan. "I'm trying to bake some bread but the oven keeps going out."

"I'm onto it," said Marcus.

It was Jack who first smelled the burning.

Angus drove an old Corolla. "You're wanting the Creative place, then?" he said, as Leila swung into the passenger seat. She hoped the thing didn't break down.

"Yes please," she said. "It's urgent. I think something's going to happen."

"We'll get there in good time," said Angus. "So are you a writer?"

"Sort of," said Leila.

"D'you like steam trains?"

"Haven't really thought about it, to be honest."

"Aye well, I'll tell you about the Strathspey Steam Railway. It's been going since..."

Leila tuned out. Trust her to hitch a lift with a steam train bore. She just wanted to be back at the Creative Hub.

"Megan, there's a problem with the lights," said Tessa.

"Aye, and what do you want me to do about it?" said Megan. Her Malcolm was still bruised and off work, and she was still mad at the woman who'd caused his injuries.

"Well, is Marcus around?"

"Somewhere."

"Could you ask him to check the fuse?"

"Ask him yourself."

"I would if…oh, forget it."

Megan went to get some herbs from the garden. She stopped outside the backdoor: something shiny was glinting on the path. She stooped to pick it up. It was a sharp knife, a workman's knife that looked as if it would double as a dagger. Who'd have dropped it there? She picked it up and laid it on the counter inside the kitchen. Then she resumed her search for herbs.

"Can you smell burning?" said Jack.

Beryl sniffed at the air. "Yes, I think I can. It's probably Max's smoke drifting in."

"Smells of plastic," said Jack. "I'll see if Marcus is around."

Marcus had put in a call to the village electrician, and now he was in the studio. After Megan's report the previous day, he thought he'd better check that nothing else was untoward. Someone had tidied up the room. He wondered if it had been Megan. The dusty floor had been swept, and there was no more trace of the room having been lived in. The surfaces all looked clean and the rubbish had been emptied. He couldn't think when she'd have had the time, but at least it was ready for the next group.

Back in the house, he found Megan squaring up to Tessa.

"What's going on?" said Marcus.

"Nothing," said Megan, casting an icy glare towards Tessa, and turning back to the kitchen. "Electrics are still playing up. Madam here's greetin' about it."

"I've called in Jimmy from the village," said Marcus. "Should have it sorted before lunchtime."

"Thanks," said Tessa.

"It's getting stronger," said Jack. "I'm sure something's burning. Let's take a look."

Had Jimmy the electrician got to the house a little quicker, he'd have found the source of the fire; but by the time he came, the library was in flames. And had he got there soon enough to investigate the shorting circuits, he'd have found the shaved wires, copper on copper, their plastic sheaths peeled away as neatly as one might peel an orange.

Chapter 30

Angus was not a reckless driver. He was law abiding, and that meant observing the speed limits unquestioningly.

"Could we not go a little faster?" Leila asked on a particularly empty stretch of road.

"Speed limit's forty for a reason, Miss," Angus had replied.

Anna was pulled out of the queue for the train at Fort William.

"We've been looking for you," said the taller of the two policemen. "Time to go home. You can tell us what mischief you've been up to on the way."

Anna slung her bag over her shoulder and allowed herself to be bundled into the waiting car.

"He deserved it," was all she said.

It was half past one, and Max sat on the grass next to Tessa. He brushed his hair back from his face, leaving a sooty streak. Tessa's light linen trousers were now ruined and clung wetly to her body.

"Things started to wrong from the start, I'd say," said Max.

"Only after you arrived," said Tessa.

"I was here before you," said Max. "Reckon you're the jinx, old girl."

"We're lucky no-one died."

"Ros looked as if she wished she *had* died," said Max. "Did you see how that firefighter had to drag her out?"

"I couldn't believe Dee," said Tessa. "Did you see how she shut the rooms off and stopped it from spreading as fast as it might have done?"

"She's got balls, all right."

"Don't let her hear you saying that."

"Think I'll go and see how Leila's doing. Good of her to come back and see if we were ok. Too late, of course."

"Why couldn't the silly bitch have phoned?"

Jack and Beryl were sitting in Jack's room. Being an annex, it hadn't been touched by the fire.

"All those books," said Jack. "Crying shame."

"Do you think someone set the fire on purpose?"

"A thwarted postman? A new widow?"

"Or the girl that we all thought had gone away?"

"Probably not the postman."

Pamela had gone to the hospital with Ros. She was showing signs of being in shock and hadn't spoken since getting back from identifying Alastair. Ros wished it would all end. She was relieved when they tucked her in between crisp clean linen and knocked her out with some kind of sedative.

"You might as well go home," said the nurse to Pamela.

"Yes," said Pamela, not at all sure about where she was going or how she was going to get there.

Leon was writing his next adventure. The fire had been amazing, just like Jack's descriptions of the Blitz. He knew exactly what Major Gonzales would have done, and so he began to write it.

Marcus and Megan were in the office. Thanks to Dee's foresight, it hadn't been too badly damaged and the phone was still working. They set about organising places for the group to sleep that night.

"There's Malcolm's mother's bungalow," said Megan. A couple of people can stay there, there's room enough for two, or four if they double up. I'll just warn Malcolm to lock his collection away. Not that these folk will be interested enough to damage it."

"I've booked the Hotel rooms," said Marcus. "They've enough room for the others. Robbie said he'd be glad of the business."

"So I guess that's the end of this place for a wee while."

"It'll take a lot of work to repair it," said Marcus. "You still planning on leaving? There'll be cleaning and decorating to do."

"I don't know," said Megan. "Malcolm wants me to stay.."

"He's a good lad."

"How about you, Marcus?"

"I'll stay on for a wee while. Look on the bright side: we'll not have a worse group than this one."

"Except the poets. The poets are the worst."

Jack helped Beryl onto the train at Fort William.

"It's been lovely," he said.

"Yes," she said, taking his hand. "It *has* been lovely. Thank you."

"Shall we…?"

"Let's just see," said Beryl. She settled into her seat in the quiet first class compartment. She blew him a kiss as the train pulled away. Jack waved from the platform. He waved until he could no longer see the train. Beryl waved until Jack was a tiny dot. She gazed out of the window for a few minutes, mulling over the strangeness of this short, eventful trip. Thinking about how wonderful it was that one could still be taken by surprise, spun off balance, delighted by the unexpected. But she had a job to do, and it was as well to start it whilst the events of the past few days were still fresh in her mind. Neither Tessa, nor Max would come out of it well. She had a few good things to say about Marcus and Megan, though. Sighing, she took her laptop out of its case and set it up on her table. Beryl Wyndham, who was better known to her millions of readers as BW York, opened up a new document and began to type her expert undercover review report for the

Arts and Literature Foundation.